The charismatic Nova Scotia preacher Henry Alline and his New Light disciples profoundly affected the nineteenth-century evangelical ethos of Nova Scotia, New Brunswick, and neighbouring New England. Alline's pietistic and mystical gospel was channelled into the Free Will and Calvinist Baptist churches, but it also gave shape and substance to the region's revivalistic tradition. In his provocative discussion of religious revivals, G.A. Rawlyk argues that at the heart of these significant social movements was a collective yearning for intimacy and a desperate search for meaningful relationships. There was also a tendency, as the nineteenth century unfolded, for various Baptist preachers to assert their authority over congregations by virtually "willing" revivals into being.

Rawlyk's view is that the Baptists of Nova Scotia and New Brunswick reached the zenith of their influence during the latter half of the nineteenth century, but his often controversial analysis defines differences between New Brunswick and Nova Scotia Baptists which extend into the twentieth century.

Ravished by the Spirit does not deal merely with the distant historical past. Rather, in its emphasis on the symbiotic relationship existing between the past and the present, it raises some fundamental and disconcerting questions about the vulnerable nature of the Baptist denomination in contemporary Nova Scotia and New Brunswick. *Ravished by the Spirit* may be regarded as a historical Jeremiad which, by glancing backwards, sees the possible hope or despair of the future.

Ravished by the Spirit

RELIGIOUS REVIVALS, BAPTISTS, AND HENRY ALLINE

G.A. RAWLYK

McGill-Queen's University Press
Kingston and Montreal

© McGill-Queen's University Press

ISBN 0-7735-0439-7 (cloth)
ISBN 0-7735-0440-0 (paper)

Legal deposit 3rd quarter 1984
Bibliothèque nationale du Québec

Printed in Canada

Canadian Cataloguing in Publication Data

Rawlyk, George A., 1935–
 Ravished by the Spirit

(The Hayward lectures ; 1983)
Includes index.
ISBN 0 7735-0439-7 (cloth); ISBN 0-7735-0440-0 (paper)

1. Alline, Henry, 1748-1784 – Addresses, essays, lectures. 2.
Baptists – Nova Scotia – History – Addresses, essays, lectures.
3. Baptists – New Brunswick – History – Addresses, essays,
lectures. 4. Revivals – Addresses, essays, lectures. I. Title. II.
Series.

BX6252.N68R38 1984   286'.09716   C84-098585-1

Contents

Foreword

To quote Dr. George A. Rawlyk's own words: "Henry Alline was a man almost larger than life and he has cast a long shadow over the religious development of the New England-Nova Scotia-New Brunswick region until the present day." Because of demonstrable proof of this statement, and because Acadia Divinity College wished to mark the bicentennial of Henry Alline's death on February 2, 1784, it was inevitable that the College should turn to the person who has researched the life of Henry Alline more thoroughly than any other – Dr. George A. Rawlyk – to give the Hayward Lectures on the noted revivalist during the 1983–84 academic year.

The Hayward Lectureship is one of the most prestigious lectureships given annually on the campus of Acadia University. The lectureship was established in October 1965, and since that time such scholars as Dr. Leander B. Keck, presently Dean of Yale Divinity School, Dr. Viktor E. Frankl, Head of the Neurological Institute, Vienna, the Very Reverend the Lord MacLeod of Fuinary, Founder of the Iona Community, Scotland, Dr. Jaroslav Pelikan, Professor of Ecclesiastical History, Yale University, Bishop Stephen Neill, London, England, Dr. John Bright, Professor of Hebrew and Old Testament, Union Theological Seminary, Richmond, Virginia, and Dr. Martin E. Marty, the Fairfax M. Cohen Distinguished Service Professor, University of Chicago, have acted as Hayward Lecturers.

Dr. George A. Rawlyk, Professor of History, Queen's University, was the first Canadian scholar to be invited to give the Hayward Lectures at Acadia. It is noteworthy that Dr. Rawlyk's four evening lectures attracted the largest audience – faculty, students, visiting pastors, and lay-people – of any Hayward Lectureship in recent years. Interested people came from miles around – from the very territory traversed by Henry Alline – and listened attentively as he spoke about "Revivals, Baptists, and Henry Alline." It soon became evident to all that, through years of patient research conducted in the archives of Acadia University and elsewhere, Dr. Rawlyk had familiarized himself thorougly with the unusual life and work of Henry Alline whose itinerant evangelism was central to the development of Baptist life in eastern Canada. Throughout the lectures Henry Alline came alive before our eyes with all his zeal, tenacity, and idiosyncrasies. While we could not identify with some of Alline's characteristics and methodology, we were able, through the lectures, to sense something of his passion, his mysticism, and his relentlessness.

In his Hayward Lectures, Dr. Rawlyk demonstrated not only the thoroughness one would expect from a scholarly historian but something of his "soul affinity" with Henry Alline. There were times when Dr. Rawlyk became highly animated as he dealt with the life and work of Henry Alline, a fact that captivated his audience again and again. Indeed, the lectures kindled not only an interest in Henry Alline but in the need for spiritual renewal in our time. To hear, as we did, from the lips of an eminent historian, an appeal for a deep spirituality appropriate for our own day was a memorable event.

It is Dr. Rawlyk's contention that Henry Alline stands almost alone as one of the few genuinely mystical persons to have laboured on Canadian soil. This is why the lectures contained in this book are worthy of careful consideration. Acadia Divinity College continues to be greatly indebted to Dr. George Rawlyk for coming to us.

Harold L. Mitton
Principal and Dean

Preface

In 1973 I thought that I would, after the publication of *Nova Scotia's Massachusetts: A Study of Massachusetts-Nova Scotia Relations 1630 to 1784*, finally abandon my research interest in Henry Alline and Revolutionary Nova Scotia and begin serious scholarly work on the Upper Canadian Loyalists. As far as I was concerned in 1973, my work on Alline had led to a *cul de sac* and I was determined, moreover, to escape the long shadow that J.B. Brebner still cast over all my historical writing.

I had in my earlier work found it very difficult to come to grips with Alline's pietism and spirituality since among other things, his religiosity raised fundamental questions about the essential nature of my own Christian faith. In my attempt to escape some of the implications of my changing religious views I had turned in the late 1960s to social-psychology and intellectual history, determined to fit Alline and myself into this seemingly acceptable and sophisticated scholarly paradigm. For me, all historical writing is basically autobiographical in nature. And certainly my writing has often painfully reflected my own psychological, intellectual, and religious search for meaning and stability.

Yet, soon after abandoning Alline and Revolutionary Nova Scotia, I found that Upper Canadian Loyalism did not really capture my imagination and this fact both exacerbated my sense of frustration and my sense of academic isolation. I, therefore, welcomed the opportunity in the autumn of 1976 to reassess Alline's career when I was invited to address a Divinity Day audience at McMaster Divinity College. In the paper I prepared for the occasion, "Henry Alline and the Canadian Baptist Tradition," I underscored the fact that my earlier work on Alline had, for a variety of reasons, underestimated the importance of his religiosity and mysticism. And this reassessment of Alline persuaded me that I would never be at peace with myself until I carefully re-examined Alline's career and the impact he had both on the Maritimes and on neighbouring New England.

Preparing *The Atlantic Provinces and the Problems of Confederation* for the Task Force on Canadian Unity in 1977 and 1978 and writing with Kevin Quinn, in 1979 and 1980, *The Redeemed of the Lord Say So: A History of Queen's Theological College, 1912–1972* only served to convince me further that I was right in my determination to return to Alline. In the summer of 1980 I was finally ready to re-examine Alline and the Allinite tradition.

My Hayward Lectures, together with my *New Light Letters and Songs*, have taken shape during this three-year period. Even a superficial reading of the lectures and the *New Light* volume will reveal, I think, that I now regard evangelical religion in a radically different manner than I once did. And, furthermore, I no longer consider it to be academic suicide to view the evangelical tradition in a sympathetic yet critical way and to argue that it is essential for Canadian scholars both inside and outside the tradition to fit it carefully within the context both of Maritime and Canadian historical development. Not to do so, in my view, is both to distort the past and to distort the present.

The four lectures included in this volume are my Hayward Lectures as I presented them at Acadia University during the last week of October 1983. Only a few minor editorial changes have been made in the text. Appendices A and B contain material not discussed in my lectures but yet material crucially important as far as the contemporary relevance of my central argument is concerned. Chapter 1, "Alline's Alline," is my attempt to reassess Alline through the prism of his *Journal*. I have been afraid neither to permit Henry Alline to speak for himself nor to regard him and his message in a sympathetic yet critical manner. In Chapter 2, "Alline and New England and the Free Will Baptists," I try to argue that Alline had a far greater impact on the "evangelical ethos" of northern New England than is usually realized. In particular he influenced the Free Will Baptists at a crucial moment in their religious development. In Chapter 3, "Alline, Maritime New Lights, and Baptists," I suggest that in Nova Scotia, a local manifestation of antinomianism, as well as American and British influences, together with the search for respectability, played key roles in pushing many key Allinite New Lights in the direction of the Calvinist Baptist Church. But in New Brunswick, the New Light legacy proved to be far more lasting and influential. In the final chapter "Revivalism and the Maritime Baptist Tradition" I try to show how, as the nineteenth century unfolded, Baptist revivalism evolved and how and why it lost much of its earlier New Light pietism and emotionalism. In a rather pessimistic conclusion, I suggest that the Baptists of Nova Scotia and New Brunswick are faced in the 1980s with serious problems – as serious as those confronted by Alline's generation. And the implicit suggestion is that Alline's basic pietistic and mystical message – a form of intense experiential religion – can even in the 1980s still energize religious revival and renewal.

I know that the historian is expected to be an objective critic of the past who carefully avoids – especially in the area of religious history – any temptation to be emotionally sympathetic or to link past events and contemporary realities. I have not been able to resist this temptation, despite the fact that I realize it would have been wise, in the scholarly sense, to do so. So be it.

Acknowledgements

This book would not have been written or published without the encouragement and assistance provided by Acadia Divinity College. Principal Harold Mitton asked me in October 1981 to give the Hayward Lectures at Acadia in October 1983. *Ravished by the Spirit* is based upon these Lectures and the book, moreover, is published with a generous subvention provided by the Hayward Bequest. Research grants from the Queen's University School of Graduate Studies, together with a S.S.H.R.C. Leave Fellowship, provided me with the opportunity to carry out the necessary research for this volume. Other financial support was provided by the University Consortium for Research on North America, Harvard University. Dunster House, Harvard University, during the 1981/82 academic year proved to be a home away from home and Professor William Hutchison of Harvard Divinity School gave me much needed support.

A number of scholars and friends have helped to coax this volume out of me. I shall never forget the encouragement given to me by Ms. Marlene Schoofs of Harvard University, and the assistance provided by Mr. David Bell of Fredericton, Professor Jarold Zeman of Acadia Divinity College, Professor Donald Akenson of Queen's, Professor Carman Miller of McGill, and Mrs. Pat Townsend, the Archivist of the Acadia University Archives. Ms. Joan Harcourt has sensitively edited the volume and Mr. Kevin Quinn, yet once again, has prepared an index for one of my books.

My wife Mary has not read a single line of this volume; yet the book is dedicated to her. Alline's androgynous God would have appealed to her.

1

Alline's Alline

Henry Alline was a man almost larger than life and he has cast a long shadow over the religious development of the New England–Nova Scotia-New Brunswick region until the present day.[1] His contemporaries regarded him as Nova Scotia's George Whitefield – as a powerful instrument of the Almighty, charismatic and uniquely spiritual. Historians in the nineteenth and twentieth centuries have been, almost to a person, overwhelmed by Alline's mystical theology, his creative powers, and his unusual ability to communicate to others his profound sense of Christian ecstacy.

I

Alline was born in Newport, Rhode Island, in 1748 and moved in 1760 with his parents to Falmouth in the Minas Basin region of Nova Scotia. Like most young people in the settlement he was brought up in a pious and Calvinist atmosphere. There was little in his rural upbringing in Nova Scotia that would even suggest that Alline would develop into the province's most gifted preacher and most prolific hymn-writer.[2] He was widely known in his community only because of his outgoing personality and his skill in "the art of tanning and currying."[3]

In the early months of 1775, the twenty-seven year-old Alline experienced a profound spiritual and psychological crisis – a crisis that when resolved, would provide the turning-point in his life. Alline's conversion – his traumatic "New Birth" – was significantly shaped by his finely developed morbid introspection, his fear of imminent death, and by the considerable pressure he felt to commit himself one way or another during the early months of the American Revolutionary struggle. Alline's conversion, it should be stressed, was the central event of his life and he felt compelled to persuade others to share in his spiritual ecstacy. One perceptive nineteenth-century observer noted that Alline was "converted in a rapture; and everafter he sought to live in a rapture; and judged of his religious condition by his enjoyments and raptures."[4]

It is noteworthy that Alline's graphic description of his conversion experience captured the attention of William James who, in his *Varieties of Religious Experience*, published in 1916, used it as a "classic example" of the "curing of a 'sicksoul'."[5] Alline noted in his *Journal*:

February 13th, 1775, when about midnight I waked out of sleep, I was surprised by a most alarming call as with a small still voice, as it were through my whole soul; as if it spoke these words, How many days and weeks, and months and years has God been striving with you, and you have not yet accepted, but remain as far from redemption as at first; and as God has declared, that his spirit shall not always strive with man, what if he would call you no more, and this might be the last call, as possibly it might be; what would your unhappy doom be? O how it pierced my whole soul, and caused me to tremble in my bed, and cry out for a longer time. O Lord God do not take away thy spirit! O leave me not, leave me not; give me not over to hardness of heart, and blindness of mind.[6]

For over a month Alline struggled to find peace of mind – or as he put it – "to be stripped of self-righteousness." And then, just when it seemed that he had reached the mental breaking point, he experienced what seemed to him to be the profound delights of spiritual regeneration. He described the beginning of his conversion experience in this way.

... O help me, help me, cried I, thou Redeemer of souls, and save me or I am gone for ever; and the last word I ever mentioned in my distress (for the change was instantaneous) was, O Lord Jesus Christ, thou canst this night, if thou pleasest, with one drop of thy blood atone for my sins, and appease the wrath of an angry God. ... At that instant of time when I gave up all to him, to do with me, as he pleased, and was willing that God should reign in me and rule over me at his pleasure: redeeming love broke into my soul with repeated scriptures with such power, that my whole soul seemed to be melted down with love; the burden of guilt and condemnation was gone, darkness was expelled, my heart humbled and filled with gratitude, and my will turned of choice after the infinite God. ... Attracted by the love and beauty I saw in his divine perfections, my whole soul was inexpressibly ravished with the blessed Redeemer ... my whole soul seemed filled with the divine being.[7]

As far as Alline was concerned, the black gloomy despair of his acute depression and morbid introspection had been miraculously removed. "My whole soul," he proclaimed

that was a few minutes ago groaning under mountains of death, wading through storms of sorrow, racked with distressing fears, and crying to an unknown God for help, was now filled with immortal love, soaring on the wings of faith, freed from the chains of death and darkness, and crying out my Lord and my God; thou art my rock and my fortress, my shield and my high tower, my life, my joy, my present and my everlasting portion.[8]

The sudden, transforming power of spiritual regeneration – the New Light New Birth – compelled Alline to declare:

O the infinite condescension of God to a worm of the dust! for though my whole soul was filled with love, and ravished with a divine ecstasy beyond any doubts or fears, or thoughts of being then deceived, for I enjoyed a heaven on earth, and it seemed as if I were wrapped up in God.[9]

These emotionally charged words would provide the cutting edge of his Christian message until his death in 1784. Over and over again in his *Journal* and published sermons and pamphlets and his hymns and spiritual songs Alline referred to his having been "ravished" by the "Divine ecstasy," and also to his having been "married" to his Saviour by the redeeming power of the Holy Spirit. Divine love had overwhelmed him to such an extent that he viewed his own experience as being the pattern set for all others. It is not surprising, therefore, that Alline expected his followers to share the intense ecstasy of spiritual rapture – the central New Light experience – which he himself had so recently experienced and which he regarded as being the only satisfactory means of regeneration.[10]

Alline's traumatic conversion was obviously the critically important event of his life and this point merits repetition. His description of it in his *Journal*, available and distributed in manuscript form as early as 1789 and in print in 1806 and in his *Two Mites Some of the Most*

Important and much disputed Points of Divinity, first published in
Halifax in 1781, provided the pattern for his disciples to appropriate,
and to emulate. Alline was eager to generalize from the experience of
his particular conversion and to make it the universally accepted
evangelical norm. His audacity – some would call it "spiritual arro-
gance" – appealed to many Nova Scotians who were certainly confused and disoriented by the divisive forces unleashed by the American
Revolution.

It should be stressed that, according to Alline, the Scriptures and his
own mystical experience had convincingly showed him that Calvinism
was a pernicious heresy. "The lesson, why those, that are lost, are not
redeemed" he declared "is not because that God delighted in their
Misery, or by any Neglect in God, God forbid." Rather it resulted "by
the Will of the Creature; which, instead of consenting to Redeeming
Love, rejects it, and therefore cannot possibly be redeemed." "Men and
Devils" he asserted "that are miserable are not only the Author of their
own Misery," but they also act "against the Will of God, the Nature of
God, and the most endearing Expression of his Love."[11]

In a particularly evocative poem inserted in his *Anti-Traditionalist,*
first published in Halifax in 1783, Alline attempted to crystallize the
essence of his theological position. He realized that many of his readers
would remember his poetry and hymns long after they had forgotten
his sometimes opaque and disjointed theological writing:

> But let me turn, and with my Reader gaze
> Once more with wonder on the bloody Scene;
> Raised with the Cross they give the sudden Plung[e].
> To Rack his Frame sag on the ragged Nails,
> O how! good God, how canst thou yet survive!
> And why my Soul, why all this Rack of Woe?
> It is for me the God of nature Growns?
> How can I write? or dare forbear? I gaze!
> I'm lost! I believe, then doubt, the Scene so strange
> My faith is staggered by the stoop so great;
> And yet again I feel, and must believe;
> It must be true; its like the God I own.

And near your Hearts, O reader waits the same,
Knocking with his endearing Charms of Love.
O hear, receive and feel the sacred Truths!
Give him thy Sins, receive his Grace then shall
This Christ, the Conquest, and the Crown, be thine;
And then eternal Ages speak his Worth. ...
But O he hangs yet on the bloody Cross
And Groans methinks, I hear but Groans for who?
For you and me, O reader, see him Dye,
And in his Death make sure eternal Life;
And from his Groans immortal Songs of Joy. ...
Listen O Heavens and hear ye Sons of Men.
"Father Forgive them" Cries the dying Lamb;
The Bleeding Victim in the pangs of Death.
Say O my reader dost thou hear the Cry?
Or canst thou stand against such melting Love?
And O he dies! but no my Saviour lives.
Ah lives for me, and lives to die no more.
Rejoice ye dying Sons of men, he lives,
And Crowned with all your sins, ye Mourners Crowd,
Ye sinking Millions to his Courts of grace;
His grace is free, and all is done for you;
Ye've seen him wade throu' all your guilt and woe
In seas of Blood thro' all his Life, or Death
A ling'ring death thro' all his servile walk
From the coarse Manger to the Blood Cross:
There won the Field in Death, then tower'd aloft
With Scars of honour to the realms of Light,
To spread for you the Gates of endless Day,
And court you to the Mansions of Delight.
O what displays of ever lasting love!
Free grace the news; free grace the lasting Song,
Free grace to Jews and to the Gentile throng;
Free grace shall be the ever lasting theme;
Jehovah's product, and Jehovah's fame;
Goodness his nature, boundless love his name.[12]

Alline's "Radical Evangelical" and New Light message, it is clear, in its essentials at least, reflected what Professor Stephen Marini has sensitively referred to as "the distinctive elements of the Evangelical tradition ... intense conversion experience, fervid piety, ecstatic worship forms, Biblical literalism, the pure church ideal, and charismatic leadership."[13] And Marini correctly locates Alline at the heart of this Whitefieldian New Light framework. But there was also, of course, an important heterodox element in the volatile mixture making up Alline's theology. And many of Alline's contemporaries were aware of the potentially explosive nature of his highly mystical theology. In a particularly discerning critique of Alline's theology, the Reverend Matthew Richey, a Nova Scotia Methodist, pointed out that the Falmouth preacher's "tenets were a singular combination of heterogeneous materials derived from opposite sources."[14]

Henry Alline, it is clear, was not only a transmitter of what was often referred to as the "Whitefieldian sound," but he was also able to perceive a special purpose for his fellow Nova Scotians in the midst of the disorienting American Revolutionary situation. He became, I have argued elsewhere, the charismatic leader of a widespread and intense religious revival which swept the colony during the war years. "The Great Awakening of Nova Scotia" was, without question, one of the most significant social movements in the long history of the colony. It was, among other things, the means by which a large number of Nova Scotians – especially the so-called "Yankees" – extricated themselves from the domination of neighbouring New England which they had left a decade and more earlier. By creating a compelling ideology that was specifically geared to conditions in the isolated northern colony, Alline enabled many Nova Scotians to regard themselves as what Gordon Stewart and I once called *A People Highly Favoured of God*. These people were provided by Alline with a unique history, a distinct identity, and a special destiny. A new sense of Nova Scotia identity, we have argued, had clicked into fragile place – to replace the disintegrating loyalty to New England and the largely undermined loyalty to Old England. But this was not all that Henry Alline accomplished. At one time I thought that it was and then I re-read his

Journal and his *Hymns and Spiritual Songs* and *Two Mites* and *The Anti-Traditionalist*. It is clear to me now that Alline also preached the simple, emotional Whitefieldian evangelical gospel of the "New Birth" – without its Calvinism – and thus provided a powerful new personal and spiritual relationship between Christ and the redeemed believer in a world where all traditional relationships were falling apart. Alline was, it is clear, obsessed with the mystical relationship of Christ with regenerate man, and because of this preoccupation he was able to use his charismatic powers to drill the reality of this insight into the minds and hearts of his thousands of Nova Scotia listeners. He was obviously a man who was especially sensitive to disintegrating relationships and one who therefore could relate to his fellow Nova Scotians who, too, were preoccupied with disintegrating relationships. For Alline, a personal relationship to Christ was the means of resolving all the difficulties arising from a myriad of disintegrating human relationships. Conversion was thus perceived as the short-circuiting of a complex process – a short-circuiting which produced instant and immediate satisfaction, solace, and intense relief.

Eventually Alline visited almost every settlement in Nova Scotia, then inhabited by approximately 20,000 people, 60 percent of whom were recently arrived New Englanders. And Halifax and Lunenburg were the only major centres of the colony unaffected by the revival Alline helped to articulate into existence. The Lunenburg area was peopled by "Foreign Protestants" who understood neither Alline's brand of Christianity nor the patriot ideology of independence. Their loyalty was a mixture of self interest, indifference, and splendid isolation. In Halifax, economic and military ties with Great Britain, together with the heterogeneous nature of the population and the influence of the elite, created a consensus violently opposed both to Revolution and to Henry Alline and his evangelical gospel.[15]

Almost single-handedly Alline was able, by his frequent visits to the settlements, to draw the isolated communities together and to give them a feeling of fragile oneness. They were sharing a common experience and Alline was providing them with answers to disconcerting and puzzling contemporary questions. For Alline, the Nova Scotia revival was, among other things, an event of world and cosmic significance. The social, economic, and political backwater that was Nova Scotia had been transformed by the revival into the new centre of the Christian world. Nova Scotia had replaced New England as the "City on a Hill."[16]

In his sermons preached as he criss-crossed the colony, Alline developed the theme that the Nova Scotia "Yankees," in particular, had, because of the tragic backsliding of New England, a special predestined role to play in God's plan for the world. It must have required a special effort for Alline to persuade many Nova Scotians that they were performing a special world role. But Alline, drawing deeply on the Puritan New England tradition that viewed self-sacrifice and frugality as virtues, contended that the relative backwardness and isolation of the colony had removed the inhabitants from the prevailing corrupting influences of New England and Britain. As a result, Nova Scotia was in an ideal position to lead the world back to God. As far as Alline was concerned, the revival was convincing proof that the Nova Scotians were "a people on whom God had set His everlasting Love" and that their colony was "as the Apple of His Eye."[17]

It would be quite wrong to stop at this precise moment – as I once did – in analyzing Alline's ideology and gospel. This point needs to be underscored. Henry Alline's preaching was certainly permeated with what has been called a peculiar Nova Scotia Sense of Mission. He was certainly concerned with the special place his fellow colonists had in the cosmic and secular drama then unfolding in the New World. But of greater importance, as far as Alline was concerned, was individual salvation – bringing Nova Scotians into a deep and personal spiritual relationship with Jesus Christ. If one cuts to the heart of Alline's thought and preaching, it is clear that his conceptual framework and his rhetoric were surprisingly similar to that put forward by George Whitefield and hundreds of his disciples. Of course, in many respects, Alline would go much beyond the Whitefieldian paradigm, largely because of the influence of such English mystical writers as William Law and Joseph William Fletcher, the "Shropshire Saint."

Alline stressed, for example, that "all mankind were *actually* present with Adam" and that the world of nature was an emanation of God–the so-called "Out-Birth." And he refused to believe "in the vicarious sufferings of the Lord Jesus" or in the resurrection of the body.[18] Moreover, he was convinced that God had spoken directly to him and that he had actually, in a flash of insight, seen the Almighty. Yet the "New Birth" was the central reality of Alline's preaching and his theology. For Alline, genuine spiritual harmony was produced only by what he described over and over again as the "ravishing of the soul." If Alline was overwhelmed by one verbal image–it was that of the ravishing of the soul by the Almighty. It was a verbal image pregnant with dynamic meaning and one which blended the sexual with the spiritual to produce a powerful explosive mixture.

Alline drove a variety of evangelical truths into the hearts and minds of his listeners largely because of his charismatic power. And moreover, he was not afraid of triggering off deep emotional reactions in his hearers. He knew, from his own experience, that this was the only way to produce a genuine conversion.

Alline was successful throughout the Revolutionary period in cultivating and in sustaining the image of the supernaturally endowed charismatic leader. This was no mean accomplishment for a man, who until the age of twenty-seven, was widely regarded as a "chief contriver and ring-leader of the frolicks."[19] Almost overnight Alline was transformed into a spell-binding preacher, a controversial essayist, and an unusually gifted hymn-writer. In New England, Alline's hymns were almost as popular as those of Isaac Watts until 1820 and were frequently reprinted in hymnals which were widely used in the Second Great Awakening in New England.

It should also be kept in mind that Henry Alline adhered to no one particular church; he had no formal education; his family owned a marginal farm and possessed little social status. He therefore cannot be identified as a leader who derived his authority from traditional institutions or from traditional ideas. He and his followers insisted that his authority stemmed from his close personal relationship with the Almighty. His ascendancy in the out-settlements of Nova Scotia and later in northern New England was unprecedented and was not soon emulated. After 1783 a whole host of evangelical preachers, many of them Baptists like Thomas Handley Chipman, Theodore and Harris Harding, Joseph Dimock and the Mannings – Edward and James – traversed the colony but none would attain the unique exclusiveness in leadership established by Henry Alline. But they tried – some tried very hard indeed.

Alline died of tuberculosis in New Hampshire in the early morning of February 2, 1784. He had made his way to New England to bring back to the land of his birth the pristine purity of the Christian gospel. He left behind him in Nova Scotia only a fragile church organizational structure, and only one ordained New Light minister. With Alline's death, the movement he had played a key role in shaping threatened to fall apart. Enthusiasm without organizational discipline – and without Alline's special brand of charismatic leadership – merely led to exhaustion, confusion, and doubt. Only slowly were his Nova Scotia disciples able to breathe new life into the old Whitfieldian gospel as they began to try to transform what to some had become antinomian New Lights into disciplined Baptists. But this process proved to be a difficult and frustrating one – and success came only after much soul searching and much failure.

II

Just before he died, Alline gave to the Reverend David McClure, the Congregational Church minister at North Hampton, New Hampshire, his manuscript journal – some of which was still written in a form of shorthand. Alline "had begun to draw off the journal of his life in a legible hand," McClure informed Alline's father, William, on August 3, 1784, "but had proceeded but a little way in it." Before his death Alline had "expressed a desire to have the remarkable providences of God towards him made public for the good of souls." And McClure had urged William Alline to find "some judicious person who is acquainted with the characters in which he wrote" to undertake the vitally important project. Alline's father was assured that his son had been "a burning and shining light in Nova Scotia and elsewhere" and that "his christian virtues, zeal, fortitude, faith, hope, patience and resignation shone bright as the lamp of life burnt down into the socket."[20]

Alline's *Journal* was not actually published until 1806. But, it is clear that manuscript versions of the journal were circulating in Nova Scotia as early as 1789. These manuscript journals were laboriously copied as they were passed from community to community and from New Light family to New Light family. And in this process Alline's *Journal* became both a source of inspiration to his followers and also a guidebook for mystical and evangelical behaviour. Alline's experiences were therefore as important, if not more important, than his often confused, disjointed and difficult theology. Nova Scotians and later New Englanders could relate to Alline as a person very much like themselves. He was one of them and each line of his *Journal* emphatically underscored this fact. If he could experience spiritual ecstacy, then they could. If he could be ravished by the Holy Spirit, they could. If he could recover from his intense morbid introspection, then they could. And if an uneducated tanner and farmer, in his late twenties and early thirties, could help to bring into existence a widespread religious awakening, then they could as well. Alline, in a very real sense, became a symbol and a popular hero; his life was convincing proof that with God all things were indeed possible.

Alline's *Journal*, in my view, is a remarkable document; and unlike Professor Gordon Stewart[21] I find it both "exciting" and evocative. In fact, I consider it to be one of the two or three most illuminating, honest, introspective accounts available concerning the spiritual travails of any eighteenth-century North American mystical evangelical. The *Journal* , in other words, is not only a significant historical document within the context of Nova Scotia development but also within the matrix of American religious life and society. Alline's Alline, the Alline revealed by his *Journal*, in my view, merits more than mere parochial interest and attention. Alline's Alline may confidently be located in the mainstream of North American religious history.

Alline's conversion in March 1775 had been extraordinarily traumatic and intensely mystical. Alline had at least been willing, as he put it, "to bow to him, to be ruled by him, to submit to him and to depend wholly upon him both for time and eternity."[22] This was the antithesis of his Yankee Calvinism; and Alline therefore delighted in bravely spitting the words "free grace, free grace!"[23] into the prevailing winds of predestination still strongly blowing across Yankee Nova Scotia. Instead of doubt, confusion, inner turmoil, Alline found that his "whole soul was filled with love, and ravished with a divine ecstacy beyond any doubts or fears, or thoughts of being then deceived."[24] He knew that he now "enjoyed a heaven on earth," and it seemed as if he "were wrapped up in God" – a God who "had done ten thousand times more for me than ever I could expect, or had ever thought of."[25] Alline went on to describe in powerful imagery the climax of his conversion.

Looking up, I thought I saw that same light, though it appeared different, and as soon as I saw it, the design was opened to me, according to his promise, and I was obliged to cry out: enough, enough, O blessed God; the work of conversion, the change and the manifestations of it are no more disputable, than that light which I see, or any thing that I ever saw. ... O how the condescension melted me, and thought I could hardly bear, that God should stoop so low to such an unworthy wretch, crying out still, enough, enough, O my God, I believe, I believe; at the same time I was ravished with his love, and saying, go on, go on blessed God in love and mercy to me, and although I do not deserve thee, yet I cannot live without thee, and I long to drink deeper and deeper in thy love. O what secret pleasure I enjoyed![26]

Less than an hour later "the Lord," Alline explained, "discovered to me my labour in the ministry and called to preach the gospel." God had spoken to him directly from the 40th Psalm; the Almighty had "put a new song" in his mouth containing "the glad tidings of salvation and messages of peace to my fellow-men."[27] Alline had been chosen to preach the gospel at a crucial turning point in his life and in the collective life of Nova Scotians. God had realized that Alline was an "unlikely" candidate; his "capacity in the world was low, being obliged to labour daily with my hands to get a living." His parents were old and Alline "had the whole care of these temporal concerns." Moreover, Alline's education – as he cogently expressed it – "was but

small."[28] Yet Alline felt a powerful call to preach the evangelical gospel
he had so recently experienced first hand; in late March 1775 there was
no fork in the road just ahead. There was only one road for Alline and
that led to the evangelization of Nova Scotia and perhaps neighbouring New England. Alline was the Almighty's instrument to bring
about fundamental change in Nova Scotia; Alline had been "ravished" by the "blessed Redeemer." He had appropriated "divine ecstacy"
and had been "wrapped up" in the Almighty in an unusually traumatic
conversion. Not only had Alline experienced God directly through "the
scriptures" – but he had also, for an eternal moment, actually felt the
divine essence – and seen the Spirit – and heard "the still small voice" of
God. In other words, his "New Birth" witnessed the blending of a rich
variety of stimulii. He "saw the word of God" in the Bible and the word
had overwhelmed him, penetrating into the deepest recesses of his
being. He heard God speaking directly to him and he could not resist
the appeal of this message. But even more than this, Alline actually felt
Jesus Christ enter his life and the only way he could attempt to describe
the intense pleasure involved was by using sexual imagery. Alline was
obsessed with the word "ravish" and he used this word over and over
again in his *Journal,* his pamphlets, and his sermons to describe the
actual moment of conversion. "Redeeming Love" he stressed, breaks
into the soul "with repeated scriptures" and with "such power." The
"ravishing" of the soul was followed by the deep satisfaction provided
by what some might call a "religious orgasm." There was a tremendous
sense of relief, "darkness" was "expelled" and the "heart humbled and
filled with gratitude" and Alline found himself "soaring on the wings
of faith, freed from the chains of death and darkness, and crying out
my Lord and my God."[29]

For Alline Christ was the "Heavenly Charmer," his "Lover," and
his "Redeemer." Alline seemed drawn to Christ, in a sense, in the
same powerful way he had been drawn to the "beautiful woman" he
dreamed about and wanted to marry. Conversion for Alline was marriage to Christ; he was now the "most beautiful object that ever I beheld"
and Alline loved him intensely and passionately and they were as one
since Alline felt himself "wrapped up in God."

It was not enough for Alline to be ecstatically converted, and this point needs to be emphasized. His conversion obviously was the means whereby the "spiritual" and "carnal" aspects of his being were integrated and the "New Birth" provided him, moreover, with a personal relationship with Christ which renewed and revitalized personal relationships which he had felt had been disintegrating. But the twenty-seven year-old tanner-farmer was eager to declare his complete independence of his parents and only becoming a full-time itinerant preacher would accomplish this goal. Alline, though in his middle twenties, was still regarded as a dependent child by his father who ordered him to family prayers, and who stressed the fact that the youngest son had a special obligation to care for his aging parents.[30] Alline felt a powerful need to escape the clutches of the parents he both adored and feared. His father represented the vindictive Calvinist God Henry had rejected, and this rejection was at the core of Alline's new-found sense of mature identity. He had escaped adolescence late in life and the process of maturation was compressed into a few days of enlightened understanding. Normally, as Erik Erikson has perceptively observed, the formulation of identity proceeds almost subconsciously as "a quiet and unspectacular adjustment to self and what lies beyond self." But there are times, rare though they may be, when, because of unusual "outer" or "inner" circumstances, the so-called process of identity formulation can approach "catastrophic proportions." At such times, and this was certainly the case in 1775 in Nova Scotia, a person like Alline was "most susceptible to the propaganda of ideological systems which promise a new world-perspective at the price of total and cruel repudiation of an old one."[31]

Erikson also maintains that one cannot "separate personal growth and communal change" nor can one "separate ... the identity crisis of individual life and contemporary crisis in historical development because the two help to define each other and are truly relative to each other."[32] What is remarkable from Alline's *Journal* is that for the pre-1775 period there is no explicit or implicit reference to any "contemporary crisis in historical development." There is no mention made of the Stamp Act Crisis, the Boston Massacre, the Intolerable Acts, or of any events or personalities involved in the transformation of

"Resistance to Revolution" in New England. It is as though Alline was either completely ignorant or completely indifferent to those powerful forces which were then converging in the Thirteen Colonies and pushing the Americans inexorably towards independence. Of course, it is always dangerous to argue from silence yet the conclusion is inescapable that Alline, by being isolated in Falmouth, Nova Scotia in the 1765 to 1775 period, had in fact missed a crucial decade of ideological development. As Professor Bernard Bailyn has contended, these years witnessed a transformation in American values. The "views men held towards the relationships that bound them to each other – the discipline and pattern of society" were all fundamentally altered and "the right, the need, the absolute obligation to disobey legally constituted authority" became the "universal cry" of the patriots. But this "universal cry" struck no responsive chord in Alline and most of his contemporaries. Alline, like many patriot leaders, had experienced a revolutionary change in attitude towards "relationships" and "the discipline and pattern of society."[33] Alline's experience, however, was not shaped by a forward looking revolutionary ideology but rather it was molded by a traditional evangelical response to crisis. Some might argue that Alline's conversion was, in fact, precipitated by his implicit and unstated concern about developments then unfolding in his former home. Confronted by Revolutionary ideology, an ideology he may not have fully understood, Alline retreated as one scholar has put it, "from the grim realities of the world to the safety and pleasantly exciting warmth" of evangelical religion.[34]

One can, of course, never be absolutely certain about motivation. What is known about Alline's conversion, however, both from his *Journal* and other writing, as well as from comments made by his contemporaries, is that it took place solely within a Falmouth, Nova Scotia context. Outside temporal events did not, in any way, impinge on his "New Birth" experience.

III

On experiencing the "New Birth," Alline felt a great need to share his new-found faith with his parents. "Surrounded by the arms of everlasting love," as he explained it, and happily resting "in the arms of redeeming love," Alline rushed down to his parents, at sunrise, to declare "to them the miracle of God's unbounded grace to me." In this act, Alline was asserting both his independence and his dependence. For the first time in his life, Alline explained to his parents what the Bible actually taught about the "love and condescension of an infinite God" and then, also for the first time, he led the morning prayers to the delight and amazement of his parents. "I had never been heard to speak even one word of my own standing," he observed, "nor ever known to pray either in public or private." Yet, Alline was afraid to tell his parents about his decision "to preach, ... keeping that in my own mind;" the "New Birth" was something his parents could quite happily accept – regarding it as an integral part of their Yankee Congregationalism. But any decision on his part to challenge the traditional role of the "educated ministry" was anathema to his mother and father. Looking back at his procrastination, Alline commented:

I have since thought, it was the work of the devil, to keep it concealed, for it kept me back from public improvement, longer than perhaps otherwise I might have done, and caused me to pass many a sorrowful hour, not knowing what to do; I having no one to tell my mind to, or ask advice from, who perhaps might have been instrumental in God's hand of helping me out, and shewing me the way of duty.[35]

While he pondered his fate, and tried to summon sufficient courage to cut his future from his parents' present and past, Alline found great pleasure in walking over the dykeland "in private for hours and hours" where he "conversed with God oftentimes as with an intimate friend, and feasted on his love." These conversations, however, did not help Alline resolve his dilemma about, what he referred to, as his "call to the ministry." Throughout the period from April 1775 to May 1776, Alline could think "of little or nothing else" but preaching his unique brand of "New Light" Christianity. At first, he was satisfied with merely witnessing to his close friends – people like his brother-in-law John Payzant. Gradually "the glorious work of God began to spread in that dark land," as Alline deflected the youthful enthusiasm of his young "frolicking" friends into religious introspection. As the revival, or the "New Light Stir," spread, Alline felt himself under increasing pressure to "come out, and attempt to speak in public." He felt that "it would have been very easy for me, believing that God would go with me;" yet Alline was also painfully aware of the "prejudices of education and the strong ties of tradition" which "so chained me down, that I could not think myself qualified for it, without having a great deal of human learning." Alline went on to point out that despite the fact that he

had not the least doubt, but God had called me to the ministry, yet I could not believe, that it was his will, that I should preach, until he had found out some way to get me qualified by human assistance, for I thought I must go, but could not go without learning, neither could I believe that God expected that I should go without it. O the strong chains of tradition, and the great prejudices of education! how many trials and heavy hours might I have escaped, if I could have believed that God would or ever could call any one to the work of the ministry, with no more human learning, that what I had.[36]

A desperate Alline, fearful that "the prime of my days would be over" before being "employed in the cause of Christ," finally summoned enough courage to talk about his problem with one of his brothers-in-law – possibly John Payzant. He wanted to be prodded into preaching; but his brother-in-law, who was also "under the chains ... respecting human learning," merely advised Alline "to apply myself immediately to reading and studying until some door opened to me to attain to more learning." Feeling in October 1775, that he had been directed by the Holy Spirit to "proceed to New-England ... to get learning there," Alline made his way to Cornwallis from where a vessel was to sail shortly for Boston. Alline carefully avoided telling his parents why he was going to Massachusetts; according to them he was sailing there in order to see relatives and also to flee from the aggressive British "press-gangs."[37]

It is remarkable that Alline, at this crucial turning point in his life, was carefully hiding his real motivation from his parents. He obviously was intimidated by them and by the religious values which they symbolized. Here was a man, almost twenty-eight years old, who had been traumatized only months before by an intense conversion experience, who could not tell his parents that he had to return to New England in order to be properly educated there for the Christian ministry. Did deference, intimidation, and fear account for Alline's peculiar behaviour – some would call it dishonesty? Why was the man who had experienced first-hand the "ecstacies of joy, praising and adoring the Ancient of Days, for his free and unbounded grace," so reluctant to explain his real feelings to his parents? There are no easy answers to these questions. It seems that Alline, like many children, could not express openly his deepest anxieties to his parents. There was a communications gap that he felt incapable of bridging and, moreover, he intuitively feared that his mother and father, fully aware of his shortcomings and vulnerabilities and powerfully attached to Congregational traditionalism, would emphatically criticize and reject his decision to become a minister of the gospel. To avoid this anticipated rejection, Alline told them nothing about his real reasons for going to Boston. Once properly educated, he could return to Nova Scotia, with his New England "learning," assuage his parents and serve his Redeemer at the same time.

In the late autumn of 1775, Alline waited in Cornwallis for the ship to set sail for Boston. But the vessel "was seized" and its owners decided to delay the voyage until the spring of the following year. Alline could not be certain if the delay had been brought about by the Devil or by the Almighty. And an outbreak of an epidemic of small-pox in the Falmouth region only served to exacerbate his anxiety and his guilt as did mounting societal pressure on him to become active in the local militia.[38]

During the winter months of 1775 and 1776, Alline's views regarding education and the Christian ministry underwent a significant change. And by April 14, 1776, he, at last, felt that he could declare his independence of his parents and all that they represented. News about the Anglo-American conflict in the Thirteen Colonies had persuaded Alline that returning to New England to be educated there no longer made any sense. Moreover, the news triggered in Alline – what the Falmouth tanner described as God's breaking "into my soul with the revivals of his grace, the sweetness of his love" –

the vanity of all things here below, and the worth of souls, which gave me such a longing desire to go forth with the gospel, and proclaim the Redeemer's name, that my soul cried out, Send me, send me, O Lord God, in thy blessed name, and take away all honour, but the glory of the cross, and all the commissions but a commission from heaven to go forth, and enlist my fellow-mortals to fight under the banners of King Jesus: and my soul rejoices to take it for my whole portion, while on this mortal stage.[39]

Christ and not George III or the patriots alone merited unquestioning allegiance and Alline was determined to be involved, not in the "inhuman" civil war, but in the cosmic battle then raging between his Redeemer and the minions of the Devil. And the Anglo-American crisis helped to shape Alline's resolve "to preach the gospel" as did some strong advice from yet another of his brothers-in-law.

His brother-in-law bluntly asked Alline "what I was waiting for?" "If God" had called him, he "ought immediately to go, and not wait for any more learning." Alline limply replied that "although I was convinced that God had called me, yet I could not think that it was his will for me to proceed, until that he had given me more human wisdom." "Why" answered his brother-in-law "has not Christ learning enough?" "Is he not able to teach you in half an hour in his school, more than you'll be able to obtain in the seats of human learning all your life?" "If God had called" him, Alline's brother-in-law continued, then "the spirit of God's" would ensure his "success." "Man's wisdom and learning" was frothy emptiness when contrasted to inspiration.[40]

Finally, on April 18 "being a day set apart for fasting and prayer," Alline met with a small group of worshippers and for the first time "came out and spoke by way of exhortation." Though he felt "some liberty," he also experienced acute anxiety, wondering whether he had made a fool of himself and had disgraced his Saviour. What made matters even worse for Alline was the realization that his preaching "was not agreeable" – as he put it – to his parents. Thinking that he "was under a delusion," they left the house of worship when he was speaking. "O how it would cut me sometimes," Alline confessed, "The greatest trials I met with were from my parents, who were so much against my improving." But despite their overt criticism, Alline persevered, preaching to his friends and neighbours "every Sabbath-day";

being sometimes in the dark and sometimes in the light; and when I was in darkness, and did not find the spirit of God with me, when speaking, I would be ready to sink, and thought I would preach no more; and when I got life and liberty again, my strength and my resolutions were renewed, and thus God dealt with me, and carried me through various scenes.

One of the most important "scenes," without question, was the enthusiastic acceptance, on the part of Alline's parents, of his role as "preacher of the gospel." "They were as much engaged for me to preach the Gospel" he proudly declared, "as I was, and would have plucked out even their eyes for my encouragement." Alline now felt himself "lifted ... above the fears and trials of the world." Alline had finally been able to declare his independence of his parents and they, in a fascinating reversal of roles, began to display a growing deference to and dependence on their son. Buoyed by this acceptance and driven by a conviction that he had only a limited time to spend in "the vale of tears," Alline was determined to preach his gospel in every settlement in Nova Scotia.[41]

News that "Henry Alline was turned New-Light preacher" drew scores of visitors to Falmouth. "Some came to hear what the babler had to say," Alline reported, "some came with the gladness of heart that God had raised up one to speak in his name; and some come to make a scoff, but it did not seem to trouble me much; for I trust God was with me and supported and enabled me to face a frowning world."[42] By early November 1776, Alline noted in the Falmouth-Horton area that "the Lord was reviving a work of grace."[43] Throughout December 1776 and the early months of 1777 Alline itinerated in the Cornwallis-Horton-Newport area – the region he knew best in the colony. When opposition to his preaching created unanticipated problems in the Cornwallis area in May, Alline decided to visit Annapolis where he saw little evidence of "the power of religion."[44]

When he returned to Cornwallis, Alline confronted two Presbyterian ministers who "inquired after my right to preach." Alline replied that his "authority was from heaven" and he was immediately attacked for preaching "without a license from a society of ministers." Alline was, moreover, criticized for "breaking through all order." When the two Presbyterian ministers discovered that Alline was stubbornly "established in my sentiments and not easily moved – they began to be more moderate, and to advise me, making me an offer of their libraries, and what assistance they could give me, if I would leave off preaching until I was better qualified." In reply, Alline "told them the Lord knew before he called me, how unqualified I was as to human learning, and as he had called me, I trusted he would qualify me for whatever he had for me to do." "Besides" Alline continued, "the work of God was the prospering in my hands, and therefore I did not dare to desert it." There was, in particular, "a considerable stir among many of the young people" in the Newport-Falmouth-Horton area. "A great number met almost every evening," he noted "and continued until eleven and twelve o'clock at night, praying, exhorting, singing, some of them telling what God had done for their souls, and some groaning under a load of sin."[45]

After visiting Annapolis early in August, Alline returned to Cornwallis and then to Falmouth which he left late in October for Newport. In November, he was back in Cornwallis and on November 20 he rode off to visit Wilmot where he "found the Spirit of God still troubling the waters, and some souls happy" despite the "very high opposition ... especially from the minister of the place, and many of his church." "O the damage that is done by unconverted ministers," Alline complained "and legal professors." "I have found them in my travels" he went on "more inveterate against the power of religion, than the open profane."[46]

IV

In February 1778, Alline experienced his first, long black night of despair and doubt. The "horror of darkness" engulfed him and "the strong bulls of Bashan have beset me around." He movingly described the "darkness and distress" of his mind and conscience:

This was the first distress, darkness or doubt of my standing that ever I had known since my conversion: for now I gave way to the enemy (it being new to me) so that I wholly doubted my standing, that I tried to invalidate all the evidences I had since my conversion of having enjoyed the presence of God, and to throw it all away: yet I found something like an anchor of hope within the veil, which I could not get rid of; though I tried much, and prayed to God to take it away. O the unspeakable distress I was under! I could neither eat, drink nor sleep with any satisfaction; for it was wholly new to me, so that I knew not what to do, what to say, where I had been, where I now was, nor where I was going. O my soul cried out to some unknown God. Help, help, O my God: if thou art mine; if not, O my God undeceive me.

For "three days and three nights (as Jonah was)" Alline found himself "in the belly of hell." He had tumbled from the mountain peak of "ravishing ecstacy" to the "bottom of the mountains, and the earth with her bars" surrounded him. Just when he seemed to be devoid of redeeming faith, the Almighty "remembered me, and brought me again to rejoice in the wonders of his love, and to triumph over the powers of darkness." When Alline was delivered from the hell of his intense doubt, he experienced "unspeakable happiness" and was "convinced it was all in great love, yea, of unspeakable benefit to fit me for the work I had before me, which God knew, though I did not."[47]

Alline's was an amazing and honest admission of agonizing doubt; he was not afraid to scrape into the inner recesses of his faith and declare to posterity both his vulnerability and his integrity. This basic and almost transparent honesty and openness helps to explain his tremendous appeal. Nova Scotians, obviously, could empathize with him and resonate with the wild oscillations of his feelings.

Throughout the summer and autumn months of 1778, as he itinerated up and down the Annapolis Valley, Alline sadly noted that the awakenings he had helped spark into existence were often quickly followed by periods of spiritual declension and sectarian conflicts.

Alline found the activities of the Baptists in the Horton area particularly annoying with their "disputes about such non-essentials, as water Baptism." When in January 1779, the Cornwallis Congregational Church offered to ordain Alline, his response was to stress that he could never "be settled in any one place; for I would rather stand wholly alone in the world, than to go contrary to the gospel."[48] And, for Alline, going "contrary to the gospel" meant refusing to itinerate as the Spirit directed him. On April 6, Alline was ordained "in a large barn" in Cornwallis as an "itinerant minister." "After prayer and singing, and a sermon preached," he "received the imposition of hands by nine delegates, three chosen out of each church," from Cornwallis, Horton and Falmouth-Newport.[49]

In late April 1779, Alline sailed from Cornwallis to the St John River where in the Maugerville area the "work of the blessed God increased" and Alline was able to breathe new life into a disintegrating church. On his return to the mouth of the river, to present-day Saint John, he was depressed with the "darkness of the place." "The greatest part of the people," he noted "as if they were to die like beasts." "I suppose" he went on "there were upwards of 200 people there come to the years of maturity, and I saw no signs of any christian excepting one solider."[50]

Sometime in June, Alline sailed to Annapolis where he "found the work of God in some degree reviving: some in distress and in some sense of their danger." But he also discovered that one of his early converts was spreading malicious rumours about Alline's sexual life. The Falmouth preacher, it was asserted, had been seen "in bed with a young woman" and Alline was now "looked on ... with coldness." Eventually, Alline's accusor confessed that "he had told a lie" and had "been imposed upon by the devil and his own malicious nature." Though he had never before endured such bitter calumny, Alline "learned to pay no regard to false reports" and used the occasion to trigger a revival of religion. There was much "travailing in the pangs of the new birth" and many nights he "sat up until twelve, one, two and three o'clock, labouring with distressed souls."[51]

When he returned to his home-base in July, Alline discovered a new kind of "distress" produced by "the enemy getting in among the christians in warm debate, and sowing discord about non-essential matters" especially "water-baptism." The "vain disputes" were such that Alline resolved in August to escape by riding down to Annapolis. En route he penned the following brief poetic prayer:

> Take me, send me, O thou indulgent God,
> To spread the blest Redeemer's love abroad:
> Send me, O God, the gospel trump to blow,
> To mortals dead in sin, and doom'd to wo,
> That they may know thy love, before too late
> They rue in darkness their eternal state.

In the Annapolis-Granville region, Alline found "the society still engaged in the cause of God: but many scoffing, making their bands strong." Seeing little evidence of the Spirit's work, Alline resolved in late August to sail once again to the St John River where he was certain there would be a far more positive response to his message. He rejected on October 29 a "call to stay" as minister to the Maugerville Church, explaining, in some detail, that he had "no expectation of being called to settle over any particular church or flock." Nevertheless, he promised to visit them regularly, thus "making you the people of my particular care while present."[52]

On November 13, 1779, Alline was back in Annapolis where he "enjoyed great liberty in the gospel" despite growing and often vociferous opposition. He spent December, January, and February in the Cornwallis-Falmouth region where, he noted, "the Lord seemed to be reviving his work again." After many of his sermons, some of his audience "would arise, exhort and witness for God." Exhorting became an integral part of Alline's worship service. Men and women were encouraged to witness to their faith; but they were encouraged to do more than merely witness. They were urged to personalize Alline's evangelistic message – to dissect it into meaningful segments – and then bombard their friends with these verbal powered projections – projections which, in a sense, took upon themselves an aura of divine inspiration. Alline's message was thus powerfully reinforced and in the prisms of the exhorters' enthusiasm redirected in a myriad of directions.[53]

In early March 1780, Alline set out for Annapolis on "snow shoes" accompanied by "a young man" – probably Thomas Handley Chipman – who carried his "saddle-bags." Alline was planning to spend six months in the Annapolis region and the St John River Valley. He found up the St John River that "the work of God was not so powerful as it had been" and around Annapolis there were stultifying and divisive "disputes about water-baptism" – bitter "disputes" which had affected the entire Annapolis Valley. On returning to Cornwallis, in July, one month early, an exasperated Alline felt compelled to unburden his soul about what he conceived to be the increasingly pernicious debate "about water-baptism:"

O how much advantage does the enemy get in the minds of christians by those zealous disputes about non-essentials; making that the chief subject of their discourses when the essentials or work of God is neglected. I have often observed in the short compass of my ministry, that when the christians get much of the life of religion with the love of God in their souls, those small matters were scarcely talked of, but whenever they met their discourse was about the work of God in the heart, and what God had done for their souls; inviting sinners to come to Christ, and setting forth in their conversation the important truths of the gospel; but as soon as religion grows cold, then they sit hours and hours discoursing about those things which would never be of service to body or soul, and proving the validity of their own method or form of some external matters, and condemn others, who do not think as they do. Ah, how many hours have I seen spent even among christians to prove the different methods of water-baptism either to infants or adults, either by sprinkling or immersion; when it would not at all help the poor soul in the least out of its fallen state back to God without the true baptism of the spirit of Christ, which alone can. O that all the distinction might be made only this, to wit, christians and the world: converted or unconverted. And that the christians or children of God might go hand in hand, as if there was no difference among them, since they are all agreed in the essentials: yea me thinks every thing else is too small to be mentioned among them.[54]

Alline had perceptively realized that in the white-heat of revival, "non-essentials" were seldom talked about. But when the revival fires went out, then peripheral issues became central ones, small differences became matters of principle, and a profound sense of Christian "oneness" was replaced by what Alline called "sectarian zeal." Alline detested, it is clear, sectarian bickering about non-essentials and he longed for the "love of the meek and lowly Jesus" to "burn up and expel" the all too pervasive "stuff and darkness" which he saw was putting a brake on the revival movement.[55]

In the late summer of 1780, Alline was delighted to spark yet another revival in Falmouth and Newport but found "not much movings of the Spirit" in Horton or Cornwallis. Alline was depressed because, despite all of his entreaties, "the fallen world is sleeping, musing, rejecting, fighting and opposing all the endearing charms, cutting, chaining, tormenting and plunging themselves down deeper and deeper into the bottomless gulf of irrevocable despair."[56] Dispirited by the indifference and apathy he found in Horton and Cornwallis, Alline, early in September, once again rode off for Annapolis, where he was soon involved in a major revival and the "great blessings" attending his preaching followed him to the St John River in October and the first three weeks of November.

On November 25, 1780, Alline was back in Cornwallis where most of his time and energy was spent "in order to settle some matters in dispute, to heal breaches, and make up divisions." In early December he visited "the darkness and death" of Halifax for the first time "to commit a small piece of my writings to the press." The "small piece" was his *Hymns and Spiritual Songs on a Variety of Pleasing and Important Subjects* – a twenty-four page collection of twenty-two of his recently composed "hymns and spiritual songs."[57] The remainder of December was spent in Horton and Cornwallis where, once again, Alline found himself embroiled in heated debates about what he regarded as "non-essentials." On the last day of 1780, a morbidly introspective Alline noted in his *Journal*:

Another year is drawn to a period, and O what have I done, what advance have I made in the only thing for which I have my being? How many thousands have landed in the eternal world since this year commenced, whose die is cast and doom unalterably fixed, and I am spared? But O if I look back on the year past and review my walk, how dark and how crooked is it, and how little have I advanced my Redeemer's name and how little useful have I been to my fellowmen.[58]

Throughout the first seven months of 1781, Alline oscillated wildly between the "sweetness of that peace beyond what tongue can tell" and the "great darkness" produced by "the absence of my Lord and Master." Despite his spiritual turmoil, Alline continued to preach, hoping thereby to recapture the pristine purity of his faith.[59] He was also writing his major treatise *Two Mites* which, in late March, he delivered to his Halifax printer, A. Henry.

Alline's acute morbid introspection of 1781 was probably shaped by four important factors. First, he was writing a major theological work and literary creativity of this kind often produces introspection and self doubt. Second, he was feeling the early effects of tuberculosis – a disease which led to his early death three years later. It is well known that "alternating states of euphoria and depression" have always characterized those suffering from "consumption" as has, what has been called, a "self-driving behaviour."[60] Third, he desperately wanted to be married – to have a female friend "to lean upon." But he also felt it necessary to surrender "all up to God, let what would come."[61] And fourth, Alline, for the first time in his ministry, was confronted by "ruffians" and "military officers" who threatened him with physical abuse and who "with drawn swords ... cursed and blasphemed" him. There was much "mocking and hooting" as the British soldiers from neighbouring Windsor intimidated the famous "Yankee Neutral preacher." It is not surprising, therefore, that Alline would plaintively observe on July 6: "Yea, I found by what trials and persecutions I went through, that it was hard to have the mind in such a frame, as to suffer wholly for Christ."[62]

On July 7, perhaps in order to escape from an environment which seemed to produce too much morbid introspection, Alline sailed for the Chignecto Isthmus region of Nova Scotia. Here, among the Yorkshire and Cumberland Methodists and "Yankees" he was "blessed ... with a longing desire to spend and be spent in his blessed cause."[63] Some of his former enthusiasm was returning as was his unquestioning faith in his own redemption; there were a number of "instanteneous conversions" as women and younger people, in particular, were affected by Alline's preaching. On Sunday, August 12, Alline preached three sermons on this not untypical "Sabbeth."

and God brought some souls to Christ, and many christians to rejoice in great liberty. The hearers were so numerous, that I was obliged to preach in the fields. O how my soul travailed, while speaking, when I beheld many groaning under almost insupportable burthens, and crying out for mercy. This day the church met to receive members, and according as I had advised them, no mention was made, of what think ye of Paul, Appolos, or Cephas; but what think ye of Christ. O the power of the Holy Ghost that was among the people this day. A number joined the church, and some sinners were brought to rejoice in Jesus Christ their friend.[64]

When he left the Chignecto two weeks later, Alline was delighted to be able to report "Methinks I could say, I conversed with God as with a friend."[65]

On July 25, Alline was back at Horton after escaping, en route, from a patriot privateer. "Let them that wish well to their souls flee from privateers as they would from the jaws of hell," he stressed, "for methinks a privateer may be called a floating hell."[66] Alline found that Christ was, once again, "all my joy."

> Jesus, my Lord, I call thee mine.
> I feel thy word that makes me thine
> Now on me gird the gospel sword,
> With the whole armour of thy word,
> To spread the wonders of thy grace abroad.[67]

But Alline was disappointed with the "dead people" who came out to hear him and he felt that his message "seems to slip by them without any more impression on them, than water upon glass."[68] What a contrast with Cumberland and Alline looked longingly at the Yarmouth-Liverpool corner of the colony "where I never had been." Perhaps, here there would be a "sweetness of labouring in Christ's kingdom."[69]

V

On October 18, 1781, Alline arrived, via a "small boat," at "Cape Orsue" – present-day Yarmouth. Here he faced a furious Reverend Jonathan Scott, the Congregational minister, who "raged very high" against Alline, regarding him as a dangerous interloper. After visiting Argyle briefly, Alline made his way to Barrington, whose inhabitants he found "very dark," and then he sailed to Liverpool where he finally arrived, after being captured by an American privateer, on December 11. At Liverpool he "found a kind people, but in midnight darkness, and vastly given to frolicking, rioting and all manner of levity." Soon after, a revival began. Alline, on January 1, 1782, observed.

I preached twice every day, and the houses were crowded. Many were very much awakened; which was such a new thing (neither known or heard of among them) that many did not know what ailed them; but still thirsted to hear me speak in the name of Christ. Many would hover around me after sermon, who seemed as if they longed to speak to me and unfold their case, but dared not to open their mouths, for it was new and strange to them and to the whole town; for there never had been such a talk as a guilty conscience, a burthened mind, a hard heart or a stubborn will, or about any convictions or conversions; nor of the love of God, or declaring what he had done for their souls.[70]

On January 7, Alline left Liverpool; the previous night he had found that his "soul was full, and the truths of God seemed to pour into my mind faster than I could deliver them." He had "everything to say to the people, that I desired to, and the hearers were greatly taken hold on, and it seemed they could not go away." Alline returned on foot to

Chebogue where the Reverend Scott called him "an impudent fellow" and Alline replied by telling him that "he showed what kingdom he belonged to by his rage and malice." On February 20, Alline "set out to go on foot with two men in company" making his way to Annapolis where he arrived on March 1. One of his early converts, Thomas Handley Chipman, was preaching in the area and there was much spiritual vitality being manifested. On April 25, Chipman was ordained amidst "a vast concourse of people." Alline's brother-in-law, John Payzant, now an effective New Light preacher, opened proceedings at seven in the morning. Later in the day, Alline "preached a sermon, and then delivered the charge." It was, Alline declared, "almost like the day of Pentecost" with "some of the christians ... so carried away, that they were almost past speaking."[71]

The following day, after preaching a sermon, Alline rushed off to Windsor from which he sailed on April 29 for the St John River. Alline spent most of May, preaching twice a day, in and around Maugerville, during which time he "had happy days and much of the spirit of God moving ... among the people." On his way down to the mouth of the river on May 28, Alline had "an evening much to be remembered." He

preached about Elijah's translation, and I had such a sense of his flight, that I thought ... I should almost leave the body. O the sweet and transporting attraction that my soul felt, which carried away the old prophet that, stole in upon my heart with unspeakable joy and delight. And methinks in a degree I know and have experienced the nature and manner of his translation. Yea, never was my soul before so bore away to the realms of eternal felicity.

Early June 1782 was spent in the Chignecto region and early July in Cumberland to the east. On July 9, Alline sailed to present-day Prince Edward Island where he found only three Christians among a "very dark people" who were "openly profane." Two weeks later Alline was back on Nova Scotia soil, this time at Pictou, on Northumberland Straight. Early in August, near Truro, Alline had a bitter confrontation with two Presbyterian ministers, Reverends Cock and Smith, who called him "a strange imposter ... neither college learned, nor authorized by the presbytery." Then on August 20, Alline resolved to return to his home but before he could he "was obstructed by a sudden turn of illness" which incapacitated him for a week. On recovering, Alline found himself involved with one of the Presbyterian ministers in an especially acrimonious debate concerning original sin, predestination and the incarnation – all of which themes Alline had dealt with, in a controversial manner in his *Two Mites*. According to Alline, he had won the debate and he was therefore inspired to write on September 1, 1782:

> O Jesus, give me strength divine,
> To spread this lovely name of thine,
> While mortal life remains;
> Then shall I make thy name my song,
> Amongst the blest immortal throng,
> In heav'n's exalted strains.

Two days later, Alline was back in Falmouth.[72]

On September 30, Alline rode off to Annapolis where he "preached often and saw blessed days." Then accompanied by T.H. Chipman, Alline travelled in the direction of Liverpool. It was decided that Chipman should sail to "the river St John's" while Alline continued on to his original destination. After brief stops at Yarmouth, Barrington, Ragged Islands, and Sable River, Alline arrived at Liverpool on November 20.

Almost all the town assembled together, and some that were lively christians prayed and exhorted, and God was there with a truth. I preached every day, and sometimes twice a day; and the houses where I went were crowded almost all the time. Many were brought out of darkness and rejoiced, and exhorted in public. And O how affecting it was to see some young people not only exhort their companions, but also take their parents by the hand, and entreat them for their soul's sake to rest no longer in their sins, but fly to Jesus Christ while there was hope. One young lad ... I saw, after sermon, take his father by the hand, and cry out, O father, you have been a great sinner, and now are an old man: an old sinner, with grey hairs upon your head, going right down to destruction. O turn, turn, dear father, return and fly to Jesus Christ: with many other such like expressions and entreaties, enough to melt a strong heart.

"The work of God" Alline observed "continued with uncommon power through almost all the place." There was some "raging and scoffing, and some blaspheming" and at least one critic shouted out, during one of Alline's sermons "that is damned foolishness." An aroused Alline turned on his critic, demanded silence, and urged him "to remember what his doom would be, that dares to blaspheme the gospel of the Lord Jesus Christ."[73] Alline was not being interrupted or blasphemed but Jesus Christ was.

On January 1, 1783, Alline sailed to Halifax where he stayed for ten days; he still found that Haligonians "in general are almost as dark and as vile as in Sodom." He returned to Liverpool, for a brief sojourn, where he saw "the waters troubled, and souls stepping in." Alline then spent the first two weeks of March in Halifax and then made his way overland to Falmouth. On March 26, at Windsor, he was "taken so ill, that my life was despaired of." During most of April, May, June, and July, he remained gravely ill "and it was thought by almost every one, that I should soon quit this mortal stage." During his prolonged sickness Alline "was in divine rapture" expecting imminently to return to Paradise.[74]

He slowly regained his strength and as he recovered he became increasingly convinced that God was calling him to New England. It is impossible to be certain about Alline's motivation for visiting New England. He felt a powerful attraction, as he put it, to "go and proclaim my Master's name, where I never had preached" especially since Alline had already "preached almost all over this country."[75] Expecting to die at any minute, the Falmouth preacher felt compelled to return to his homeland in the hope of persuading the Yankees to return to the evangelical faith of their fathers.

Alline, moreover, in the summer of 1783, knew that he was dying. And he evidently wanted to die in New England. But before he died there, he first wanted "to blow ... the gospel trump." His parents encouraged him to go, expecting to meet him again only in Heaven; his friends knew that nothing they said or did could dissuade Alline from doing what he was convinced was the will of God. On August 27, he sailed from Windsor and after an unplanned stop at the mouth of the St John River reached northern Maine early in September. He would never return to Nova Scotia – to what he now regarded as his "native province."[76] He left behind him scores of disciples, hundreds of followers, and a spiritual legacy reflected in both the oral and written tradition of the religious culture of Nova Scotia and New Brunswick.

2

Alline and New England and the Free Will Baptists

Henry Alline's influence on the Nova Scotia-New Brunswick evangelical tradition was indeed significant – both in the short and long run. What is sometimes forgotten, however, is that the Falmouth preacher – perhaps indirectly – provided both spiritual shape and substance to what has recently been called the "New Light Stir"[1] – a religious revival which swept through much of northern New England between 1779 and 1781. Moreover, Alline, at a critical moment, gave to the Yankee Free Will Baptist movement, in general, and to its founder Benjamin Randel, in particular, a ready-made theological system.

I

It was a remarkable coincidence – to say the least – that in the early autumn of 1783 both Benjamin Randel and Henry Alline were preaching their respective versions of the "Free Grace Gospel" to the inhabitants of southern Maine. As he rode southward in early October, an exhausted and sick Henry Alline noted in his *Journal*

I endured vast pains and anguish of body almost every day, and was many times scarcely able to preach; but I endured it without much complaining, for I enjoyed health of soul, and was very happy at times in the Lord Jesus Christ. But as I had just got into that part of the vineyard, and saw the fields as it were white unto the harvest, I had intended (if Providence permitted) to blow the gospel trumpet through the vast country, and I could not bear the thoughts of leaving the world; although I was happy and had not the least doubt of my salvation: for I longed more than tongue can express, to be the means of bringing some of those poor souls to the Lord Jesus Christ.[2]

Just before he arrived at Brunswick, Maine, on October 17, Alline encountered some zealous but "counterfeit" revivalists who were deceiving "young christians." He chastized the immature believers for being "so fond of every thing that appears like the power of God, that they receive almost any thing that has a zeal." He then concluded with an observation permeated with fear, anxiety and perhaps prophetic insight:

I love to see preachers zealous, yea, and I believe, if they have the spirit of God, which brings meekness, love and humility with the zeal, and solemnizes the person speaking, it will not be all over as soon as they have done speaking in public, but will go with them: when those who have nothing but a spirit of self, and a false zeal ... it will be soon over, and have no solemnizing sense abiding.[3]

After spending almost four weeks preaching in southern Maine, visiting local Congregational ministers of New Light and Old Light persuasions, Alline entered New Hampshire, probably on November 13. Within five days he was in such pain – "scarcely an hour free from pain, excepting when asleep" – that he stopped writing his journal.[4] Eventually, he made his way on January 22, 1784 "very feeble" to the house of the Reverend David McClure, the Congregational minister at North Hampton, New Hampshire, where, eleven days later, he died. McClure described Alline's last few hours on earth in the following evocative manner:

By reason of his great bodily pains and longing to be with Christ, he would sometimes check himself, fearing he was too impatient to be gone. I desire, says he, to wait God's time. He said, he had begged of God, that he might not outlive his usefulness. O I long, said he, that poor sinners should have such views of the Lord Jesus, as I have. ... In the evening I observed to him that Christ was now his only help, he said, I need not to be told of that, he is now my only desire. His distress increased, and he longed to depart. I observed to him, that I trusted he would soon obtain the gracious fulfillment of the promises. I have no doubt, said he, not one, no more than if I was now there. He lay in great distress, groaning and reaching for breath. ... It was evident soon after, that his reason was going, and his broken sentences were the breathings of a soul swallowed up in God.

In this state he lay about two hours in great distress for breath, and the last intelligible sentence he spoke was. ... "Now I rejoice in the Lord Jesus."[5]

Alline would have appreciated McClure's description of his being "swallowed up in God," since, when he had been converted in early

1775 Alline had "enjoyed a heaven on earth, and it seemed as if I were wrapped up in God." "Ravished with a divine ecstacy beyond any doubts and fears," death merely and finally confirmed what Alline had once referred to as "the infinite condescension of God to a worm of the dust."[6]

Alline left with the Reverend Mr. McClure "a number of hymns, which it was his desire," according to McClure, should be published, "for the benefit more especially of his friends in Nova Scotia."[7] This manuscript was sent by McClure to Alline's namesake and cousin then residing in Boston. Two years later, in 1786, Alline's *Hymns and Spiritual Songs* was published with its 487 hymns and its 381 pages. Alline also gave McClure a manuscript copy of his journal. The *Journal* would not be published, however, until 1806.

According to McClure, Alline was "a burning and shining light in Nova Scotia and elsewhere. ... his christian virtues, zeal, fortitude, faith, hope, patience and resignation shone bright as the lamp of life burnt down into the socket." McClure added that during the months Alline had spent in New England before being "united with seraphs and saints in their pure ardours of holy and everlasting joy," the Nova Scotian had preached "with power to the consciences of sinners."[8] Many residents of North Hampton, though not ardent New Lights, were forever marked by Alline's remarkable influence. As late as 1839, for example, it was noted by the Reverend Jonathan French, one of McClure's successors, that several persons were still alive

who saw Revd Mr. Alline while at Mr. McClures. They represent every thing in his appearance and conversation as have been very spiritual and as become one just on the verge of heaven. He seemed scarcely to belong on earth. He passed the last week of his life at Mr. McClures, & preached on the Sabbath from "Zacheus come down etc." Many visited his sick and dying chamber, he had something spiritual to say to everyone. Widow Hepzibah Marston, now 95, the oldest person in the town and sister of the church, was one of his watchers the last night of his life and speaks of the prayerfulness and heavenly frame of mind with which he anticipated his departure.[9]

Fifty-five years after his death, the deeply etched image of the amazing Henry Alline could not be removed from the memory of an American like the ninety-five year old Hepzibah Marston who had spent only a few days with him. For every one Hepzibath Marston in New Hampshire, there were thousands of Nova Scotians who, as late as the 1850s, believed that Alline was indeed the "Whitefield of Nova Scotia."[10]

II

All evangelicals in New England, it should be noted, did not respond to the American Revolution as a homogeneous group. A majority, in all likelihood, regarded the Revolution as a holy war and were eager to battle for their Lord against the forces of Antichrist. A second group, sophisticated and cosmopolitan, sympathetic to the patriot cause, saw in the Revolution a God-given opportunity "to press for freedom of religious conscience" in exchange for anti-British activity. Then there was a third group – a distinct minority – who, according to a recent study, "remained neutral toward the revolution while pursuing a radically other worldly faith."[11]

Much is known about the first two groups, largely because of the work of Perry Miller, Allan Heimert, Nathan Hatch, and William McLoughlin, among others. Virtually nothing, however, has been written about the latter group – a group which obviously had so much in common with Henry Alline and his Nova Scotia followers. These evangelicals, "scattered irregularly in the hill country and along the coast of northern New England called for resolute, world-rejecting piety and renewed spiritual experience in the face of social disorder," and were suspicious of the Revolution and all that it represented.[12]

A leading member of this "neutral" or "anti-war" group was Benjamin Randel, a founder of the Free Will Baptist Church. Born in 1749 in New Castle, New Hampshire, a son of a sea captain, Randel eventually apprenticed as a sailmaker in Portsmouth and later became a tailor. In September 1770, he first heard the Reverend George Whitefield and considered him to be a preacher "having authority."[13] When Randel was on the way to hear Whitefield preach yet again he was met by a distraught messenger shouting "Mr. Whitefield is dead. He died this morning at Newbury, about six o'clock." Randel was shattered. He noted in his journal:

As soon as his the messenger's voice reached my ears, an arrow from the quiver of the Almighty struck through my heart; and a mental voice sounded through my soul. The first thoughts that passed through my mind were, Whitefield is now in heaven, and I am on the road to hell. I trembled. Every part of my body was affected, as well as my mind. My former religion appeared altogether worthless and fled from me as though it had never been. It seemed as if there never was any person so vile as I, nor anyone possessed of such heart aliena-tion, and enmity to God in all his nature. Why should I be so distressed?[14]

After two weeks of spiritual struggle, Randel experienced the "New Birth," an Alline-like conversion triggered by the death of the Calvinist Whitefield and a conversion experience which, ironically, was "univer-salistic in its concepts."[15] "The world and all its vanities are now loathsome to me," he confessed. "I hate sin and folly and have no relish for any earthly good." He went on:

What do I love? I know I love God and long after righteousness. What then is this but a change wrought by the power of God in my soul. This is conver-sion; this is what I read of in the scriptures, being born again etc. As soon as I believe this, I gave glory to God; and O! what love, joy, and peace filled my soul! Now I saw a just God and a Saviour; and, in Christ, I beheld a blessed sacrifice for sin, to the full satisfaction of Divine Justice. O! thought I, Jesus is precious to me. My soul kept crying, Jesus, Jesus. It seemed as if I had 10,000 souls, I could trust them all with Jesus.[16]

Randel then felt compelled to underscore his anti-Calvinistic conversion:

I saw in him a universal love, universal atonement, a universal call to mankind, and was confident that none would ever perish but those who refused to obey it. O, what love I felt to all mankind and wished that they all might share in the fullness which I saw so extensive and so free for them all.[17]

At first, Randel remained a Congregationalist. But by 1775 he had left this church and in the following year become a Baptist and soon afterwards was ordained a minister in that church. Though he served briefly as "a non-combatant in the Continental Army" in 1776 and early 1777, Randel by late 1777 insisted on "the priority of spiritual over temporal matters" and on the greater importance of religious revival over revolutionary activity. For his seemingly unpatriotic behaviour, he was threatened with tar-and-feathering – a punishment usually reserved for well-known Tories and Loyalists. But Randel would not be intimidated and despite all forms of harrassment he continued to preach his pietistic gospel but, as Professor Stephen Marini points out, "he had become a social pariah in the process."[18]

Randel, and others like him, endured the early years of the Revolution "in isolation, awaiting greater light from God to illumine their souls and minds." All of them, according to Marini, "shared a view of the Revolution born of their religious commitment to other-wordly realities."

War, no matter how meaningful in human terms, could not be for them more than a futile exercise in carnality, a penultimate concern that paled before the quest for spiritual enlightenment and moral purity. Whether they responded simply by deep depression and anxiety, or became seekers for the renewed presence of the spirit, or experienced new revelation through dreams, visions, and revelations, all those Evangelicals who regarded the Revolution as a merely human enterprise were driven back with renewed intensity to their religious commitment for identity and spiritual sustenance.[19]

Between 1779 and 1781, itinerating preachers in northern New England helped to set off what has been called "the largest and most intense revival and ecclesiastical expansion since the halcyon days of the Great Awakening."[20] It was called the "New Light Stir" and it seems clear that the Baptists in the region were the great beneficiaries of the revival.

Their vigorous Evangelical revivalism was a proven instrument; their suspension of educational standards for ministers provided a ready supply of clergy; their practice of itineracy and lay exhortation gave them great mobility. When religious neglect of the new settlements created a need for preaching, Baptists were most often on hand to supply it.[21]

In the "New Light Stir," the unanticipated reality of glorious military victories against the British, the "stimulus of frontier self-assertion," and the emotional enthusiasm generated by the revival, all came together in the deeply-felt conviction that Christ's return was imminent; the "Last Days" were obviously approaching – and there was a millennial spirit in the air. The revival was convincing proof that Christ was soon to return and those involved in the revival found themselves caught up in a religious drama of world-wide importance. They were, in fact, helping to accelerate historical time; they were key instruments in bringing about the "New Jerusalem." And this feeling helped fuel the revival fires as they licked up the northern valleys and jumped northwards along the Atlantic shore.

There is some evidence to suggest that the "New Light Stir" was affected, if not triggered, by Nova Scotian events and Alline's charismatic leadership. Apparently, according to a recently published study, there was a symbiotic relationship of revival in northern New England and the Great Awakening in Nova Scotia. It should be kept in mind, for example, that there is a natural tendency of "neighbouring societies, even with quite different languages" to borrow "cultural elements from one another freely."[22] This cultural osmosis was, moreover, reinforced in the New England-Nova Scotia region by a surprisingly congruent religious outlook and common social background which the inhabitants of the region shared – or at least the residents of the common northeastern frontier of New England and Nova Scotia. Since popular religion was the most significant and powerful "cultural element" at work in the region in the late eighteenth century it is to be expected that its great influence, rather than that of political ideology, was felt, despite the fact that a man like Alline was apparently unaware of it.

On May 19, 1780 the day following a lunar eclipse, all of northern New England was plunged into what has been described as "an eery and profound darkness."[23] Here was convincing proof, for many, that the return of Christ was imminent. Ezra Stiles commented in his famous *Diary*:

For several hours in the middle of the day the Obscurity was so great that those who had good Eyesight could scarcely see to read Common print; the birds and fowls in many places retired to roost as tho' it had been actually night, and people were obligated to light candles to dine by. ... During this whole time, a sickly melancholy Gloom overcast the face of nature. Nor was the Darkness of the Night less uncommon or terrifying than that of the day: notwithstanding there was almost a full moon, no Object was discernable ... thro' a kind of Egyptian Darkness which seemed almost impervious to [its] Days.[24]

Thick smoke from a huge forest fire in present-day Maine had produced the "Egyptian Darkness" in New England. But for many Yankees, including some very sophisticated ones, the "Dark Day" was further proof that the millennium was indeed imminent. And moreover the "Dark Day" seemed to push many impressionable "converts beyond the boundaries of Evangelicalism itself into millennial and perfectionist sectarianism." There was the eccentric and amazing Jemima Wilkinson who believed that she had been "spiritually and ontologically reborn" in 1777 and who as the "Public Friend," and the female Christ attracted hundreds to her unique brand of Christianity – a mixture of mysticism, prophesy, and divine healing.[25] She, however, left New England in 1782 and made her way to New York where she died in 1815.[26]

The "New Light Stir" would have more permanent impact, it may be argued, on Maine. The revival there seemed to peak in its intensity in late 1779 and in 1780. In Gorham and other communities "Men and women would commence their exhortations, and run on in the highest strain." They did this until

they wrought themselves up to complete frenzy, even to frothing at the mouth, dancing, stamping, and whirling around. These last were generally females, who would continue till they fell prostrate on the floor in a state of complete exhaustion. This was called going into a trance, or spiritual state, and as they said, holding communion with God. ... When the trance was ended, they usually came to their feet with a spring or a bound ... darting at once before some individual sinner, to whom they had a special message, assailing them with a torrent of invectives, such as calling them devils, children of the devil, sinful, lustful, artful devils, men of sin, anti-Christs; not forgetting to remind the poor culprit of each and every known fault, or deviation from the path of right, which he had been known to take from infancy up.[27]

And like the followers of James Davenport thirty years earlier, and like the New Dispensationalists of Nova Scotia in the 1790s and first decade of the nineteenth century, they vociferously attacked all manifestations of "worldliness." "Ribbons, ruffles, jewelry, and ornaments of all kinds were in their estimation especial articles of temptation used by the devil to work evil and ruin the soul of the wearer," and consequently many of them "would rise up, strip of[f] ruffs, ribbons, and jewelry, trample them under foot, or go to the door, and cast them to the devil, their owner, and in a loud voice tell Satan to take his temptations to himself."[28]

By late 1780 not only in Maine, but throughout northern New England, the revival fever began to abate. Extremism, the counter-offensive organized by the opponents of the revival, and the great difficulty in sustaining for any length of time the white-heat intensity of collective spiritual enthusiasm all combined to brake the movement. It is noteworthy that the concluding months of 1780 in much of Nova Scotia also witnessed the sudden decline of Awakening fervour. An excellent graphic illustration of this phenomenon is to be found in the church records of the Cornwallis and Horton Baptist Church. Located in the heartland of the Awakening near Alline's home, this church sensitively reflected the powerful social movement that engulfed the entire colony during the American Revolution. In the last two months of 1778 five young women and four young men were converted, "related their Christian experience," and were baptized. From January 2 to the end of June 1779, there were twelve women converts and ten male converts; then, during the latter half of 1779, seven men and nine women experienced the "New Birth." During the first four months of 1780 there were only three women converts and from May 1 to October 7 there were six women, and ten men and for the remainder of the year, none. There was not one new convert in 1781, only one woman in 1782, and a total of two women and one man in 1783 and a single man in 1784.[29]

The "New Light Stir" of 1779 and 1780, despite its relatively short time-frame, had encouraged, among other things, the growth of religious "pluralism on an unparalled scale." And in the temporarily "superheated environment" of northern New England "even the binding powers of doctrine and tradition which undergirded Evangelical Calvinism began to give way."[30] Thus the revival prepared the way for denominational competition and it also influenced the development of a religious world view – a natural outgrowth of Whitefieldian evangelicalism – which view facilitated the growth of the Free Will Baptists, the Universalists, and the Shakers.

Benjamin Randel participated in the "New Light Stir" and he also took full advantage of the remarkable way in which it had helped to reshape the New England theological landscape. In July 1780, Randel found himself "disfellowshipped" by his local Baptist Church and eager to preach the gospel. But he was torn between the "Calvinism" of his youth and his Yankee heritage and the Free Will enthusiasm of his conversion experience. "I was in great trial of mind" he observed in his journal "and in order that I might not be discovered by any, I walked into a remote place, where I had a piece of corn growing, and went into the midst of it." He felt his soul to be "in great agony." Randel then

sat down upon a rock and was praying to my heavenly Father to be taught. All at once, it seemed as if the Lord denied to teach me. This increased my trial, and I cried, Lord why may I not be taught? And the answer was, "because thou hast too many right hands, and too many right eyes." I said, "Lord, what are my right hands and right eyes?" And it appeared to me that they were my traditions, which I still held, and my brethren whom I had come out from. ... I saw, too, that I was too much incumbered with natural connexions. I saw that I needed much purifying and refining. I said, Lord, here I am, take me, and do with me as thou wilt. I freely surrendered myself, that moment into his hands.[31]

On surrendering himself, yet again, to the Almighty, Randel then experienced "the flaming power" which "instantly passed" through his soul. It was impossible for him to convey "an adequate idea" of the experience, for it was "so amazingly powerful, and began to strip away everything from me, in such a manner, that I thought I was going to lose all I ever had." Then the Holy Spirit – or "something whispered in my soul, saying, Didst thou not resign all?" Randel replied "Yea Lord, and here I am:"

The power then increased in my soul until it stripped me of every created thing, as to my affections. I tried to recollect my brethren and my connections, but I could not get any feeling sense of them. I had no feeling of any thing, but the great and awful, terrible and dreadful majesty of God, which sunk me, as it were, into nothing.

After being thus "stripped" and being forced into a state of black, helpless, nothingness, Randel "saw a white robe brought and put over me, which covered me all over." He glanced "down all over me" and he "appeared as white as snow." Then

A perfect calm, an awful reverence and a solemn fear of God, pervaded all my soul. A bible was then presented before the eyes of my mind, and I heard a still, small voice saying, look therein. I looked in at the beginning of Genesis and looked out at Revelation. I saw all the scriptures in perfect harmony; and those texts, about which my opposers were contending, were all opened to my mind.[32]

In an intense flash of divine revelation, Randel had the essential universalist experience of his regeneration confirmed. He saw that the

Word of God "ran in perfect connection with the universal love of God
to men – the universal atonement in the work of redemption, by Jesus
Christ, who tasted death for every man – the universal appearance of
grace to all men, and with the universal call of the gospel."[33]

Suddenly, Randel regained human consciousness – still sitting on the
rock "all flowing with sweat" and "so weak I could hardly sit up." He
then glanced at the location of the sun and discovered that he "had been
in this exercise as much as one and a half hour" and that he "never could
tell whether I was in the body or not."[34] All that he knew was that God,
in his wisdom, had reached down to rural New Hampshire and had
severed "the Gordian Knot of election and reprobation" which had so
perplexed and disconcerted him and his followers. Instead of the dead
hand of Calvinism there was universal love and grace available to
everyone who wished to be saved from eternal damnation.

In theory, Whitefieldian evangelicalism stressed the importance of
predestination. But, in fact, in the rhetoric of the evangelical tradition
the impression was explicitly created that each person was responsible for his or her own salvation. The "New Birth" involved two people, Christ and the sinner – and both had to reach out and touch and
thus produce the spark of conversion. The legacy of Calvinism would
never be easy to jettison; yet the outer limits of Whitefieldian
evangelicalism were flexible enough to include both predestination and
universalism. The essential litmus test for the evangelical preacher was
whether or not he could bring about conversion. For too long, scholars
have overemphasized the fundamental differences existing between the
advocates of these two opposing positions. At the leadership level,
there may have been a wide and unbridgeable chasm. But at the more
popular level, it seldom was a major impediment to revival. Free
Will Baptist preachers and Calvinist Baptist ministers could receive
enthusiastic receptions from the same communities largely because they
were preaching the same evangelical gospel and using the same
evangelical language. Later doctrinal differences might emerge as
various people stressed those small things they did not have in common in order to carve out a greater degree of self-identity and self-
importance.

By late 1780, Randel and other Baptists had broken away from their "parent Calvinist group" stressing instead "Free will principles." Throughout northern New England, during the latter years of the Revolutionary war, Randel discovered that the "New Light Stir," the work of hosts of itinerating ministers, a widespread acceptance of emotionalism and mysticism at the popular level, had all "prepared the ground" for his "message of free salvation."[35] As might have been expected, Congregationalists and Regular Baptists regarded the Free Willers as "wolves in sheep's clothing." Randel and his disciples took creative advantage of situational schimatic pressures in a variety of communities and directed them along Free Will Baptist lines.

There was, despite its universalism and Free Will emphasis, what contemporaries referred to as the "old Whitefield sound"[36] in Randel's preaching. The same point was frequently made as well about Alline's message. And like Whitefield, Randel and his associates loved to itinerate – crisscrossing Maine, New Hampshire, and northern Massachusetts frequently and regularly. Yet despite their concern about isolated and leaderless congregations, little could be done during the formative years of the Free Will Baptist movement to consolidate in any effective organizational manner the fruits of revival. It was realized that despite the heroic work of Randel and others, endemic discord would intensify until there was "a coherent social design that facilitated theological agreement, financial coordination, and disciplinary cooperation." Randel was particularly sensitive, as early as 1782, to the threat posed to his movement by "the Shaker delusion."[37]

Needing some doctrinal and organizational cement to keep the diverging elements of his movement together, Randel had prepared "such articles and such a covenant as I thought would do" for his New Durham church. The Articles, consisting of thirteen items, followed the usual New England Baptist pattern, apart from the replacement of the one referring to predestination with one asserting "freedom of the will and universal atonement." The Covenant was a concise and lucid understatement of the Free Will Baptist position:

We do now declare that we have given ourselves to God; and do now agree to give ourselves to each other in love and fellowship; and do also agree to take the scriptures of truth for the rule of our faith and practice, respecting our duty toward God, our neighbors, and ourselves.

We do promise to practice all the commands in the New Testament of our Lord and Savior Jesus Christ, so far as they are now, or shall be made known to us by the light of the Holy Spirit of truth, without which, we are sensible, we cannot attain to the true knowledge thereof. We also promise to bear each other's burdens, and so fulfill the law of love, which is the law of Christ. We do further agree to give liberty for the improvement of the gifts of the brethren, and to keep up the worship of God, and not to forsake the assembling of ourselves together, as the manner of some is. We do likewise further agree not to receive any person into fellowship, except they give a satisfactory evidence of a change in life and heart; and also promise to submit to the order of the Gospel as above. Amen[38]

Then late in 1783, because of the rapid growth of the Free Will Baptists in Maine, Randel encouraged these and other churches to meet quarterly in order:

to ascertain the state of the churches – consult upon the general interests of religion – adjust difficulties – inquire into the fellowship of those present – examine candidates for ministry, and ordain them if advisable – and engage in public worship and the celebration of the ordinances.[39]

In almost every respect, the Free Will Baptist quarterly meetings resembled the Separate Baptist associations. They were advisory in nature "Utterly disclaiming superiority, jurisdiction, coercive right, and infallibility."[40] However, they did provide opportunities for Free Will leaders and others to have fellowship with one another, to share common problems and to find common solutions. A loose, yet effective, uniformity was sought rather than divisive anarchy. Attacked from the extreme left by committed Shakers and from the extreme right by rejuvenated exponents of traditional Congregationalism, and furiously battling the aggressive Calvinist Baptists and growing numbers of Methodist enthusiasts, the Free Will Baptists tried to impose some order on what seemed to many to be their vulnerable and fragile "outposts of enlightenment."

III

Not only in the area of church polity, broadly defined, it must be stressed, did Randel feel especially threatened by competing groups. He also felt extremely vulnerable in the area of theology. It is noteworthy that until his death in 1808, neither Randel nor any of his lieutenants produced a "published work devoted to an exposition of theology."[41] This "paucity is startling" observes Norman Allen Baxter, in *History of the Freewill Baptists*, "when we recall that Randel separated from the Calvinistic Baptists for theological reasons."[42] In a sense, Baxter is right, "the paucity is startling" when one takes into account the scores of theological treatises published during these years by men with a lot less to say and also by men who lacked Randel's creativity, sense of urgency, and native intelligence. But in yet another sense Baxter is wrong. For the Free Will Baptists had their own theologian – he was Henry Alline. And there was consequently no need for them, in the formative period of their movement, to find one of their own number to formulate both a positive assertion of "Free Grace" and also a powerful critique of Calvinism. For Alline had already accomplished this in his *Two Mites* and *Anti-Traditionalist*, and in his three published sermons and in the manuscript hymns which he brought with him to New Hampshire late in 1783.

During the early months of 1783 Randel was experiencing, what his biographer described as a "very trying season."[43] He was "violently seized by a fever, which ran so high, that his life was despaired of." Once recovered, he had to work day and night at his tailoring and his farming "to maintain my little family" and to "redeem time to travel and preach Jesus to poor sinners." Then on September 26, he set out for Maine. Nineteen days earlier, Henry Alline had left Nova Scotia for the same northern frontier region of Massachusetts. Randel, "deeply impressed to go further east" made his way to the Damariscotta River, and then along to Bristol. And "after labouring a short season" in this locality "he returned homeward" stopping along the way in Brunswick and Harpswell.[44] The Free Will Baptist preacher was not reunited with his family in New Hampshire until November 22.

Despite the fact that they visited Maine at the same time in 1783 and despite the fact that they preached to some of the same congregations and traversed the same roads, there is no available and explicit evidence that Randel and Alline ever met. That Randel was aware of Alline and his theological work there is absolutely no doubt; that Alline was totally ignorant of Randel there is little doubt. The Nova Scotian always noted in his *Journal* the names of ministers he had met and, moreover, he frequently discussed the theological views of such men. In his *Journal*, Alline neither referred to Randel nor to his Free Will Baptist movement – despite the fact that their basic theological views had so much in common. And when Alline was buried on February 3, Randel played no role whatsoever in the funeral service.

Yet sometime during the early months of 1784, Randel became directly acquainted with Alline's writing. There is some evidence to suggest, moreover, that Randel's own journal accounts of his spiritual travails and the actual language he used were based upon Alline's *Journal*. The Reverend I.D. Stewart, in his official *History of the Free Will Baptists*, published in 1862, noted that at the September quarterly meeting "convened at Edgecomb, Me.," there was a determined "first effort to bring the power of the press into the service of the church." He explictly referred to "Henry Allen, a New Light preacher from Nova Scotia," who had come "into Maine, bringing with him a work of 250 pages, written by himself, and called 'Two Mites,'" in which he discussed several theological questions, such as the Fall of Man – His Recovery by Christ – Embassadors of Christ – The Power of Ordination – The Church – and the Day of Judgement." Stewart then enigmatically commented that "Both the man and the book were favourably received, as it was voted to try and have brother Henry Allen's 'Two Mites' reprinted."[45] How Alline "the man" had been "favourably received" by the Free Will Baptists was never discussed by Stewart. Some might argue that Stewart merely telescoped events; in referring to the

September 1784 quarterly meeting he really meant to refer to an earlier meeting. There was a quarterly meeting, it is true, on December 6, 7 and 8, 1783 in Hollis, Maine, but at this time Alline was totally incapacitated in the Falmouth area "by his sickness and pains" and he was expecting to die at any moment. There was another quarterly meeting, held during the first week of March 1784. Alline, who had been dead for over a month, could not, of course, have attended this meeting.

We know that Alline proudly carried with him to New England printed copies of his *Two Mites*, his *Anti-Traditionalist*, his three published sermons, and also, in manuscript form, "a number of hymns, which he had prepared to be published." And in addition, of course, there was also his journal, part of it still written in a form of shorthand.

Alline's manuscript hymns, as mentioned above, were sent by McClure to Alline's cousin in Boston and, in 1786, they were published as *Hymns and Spiritual Songs*. Nine years later in 1795 a new edition was produced by the Free Will Baptists and two years later it was yet again reprinted, this time with a new hymn included, "A Call to Sinners" written by Benjamin Randel, as well as some of McClure's description of Alline's last days on earth. There was a fourth and final edition published in 1802. Eight years earlier a tiny volume of Alline's hymns, first published in Halifax (probably in 1781) was reprinted in Windsor, Vermont. There were only twenty-two hymns in this slim volume – none of which was memorable and all of which provided convincing proof that Alline could indeed do better. Thirty-eight of his hymns were reprinted in Smith and James' widely used, *Hymns Original and Selected*. But of Alline's more than 500 hymns, only one has survived in modern collections – "Amazing sight the Saviour stands."[46]

It has been perceptively observed that the "appearance of two editions of Alline's *Hymns* within two years is evidence of the popularity of their sentiments among the Free Baptists."[47] Alline's hymns, obviously, were "widely known and popular" in the New England – Nova Scotia – New Brunswick area during the 1786–1815 period and beyond. His hymns and spiritual songs, sung to lively popular tunes, appeared at precisely the moment the "Revival of Singing" was sweeping New England and the Maritime region of British North America. In addition, and this is of crucial importance, for many residents of the region, Alline's hymns were the means whereby they could both express and define their evangelical religious views and their neo-Whitefieldian heritage.

Even though the March 1784 Free Will quarterly meeting resolved to reprint *Two Mites* immediately, *Two Mites* was not, in fact, reprinted until 1804 – twenty years after the original decision was made. "All of the sentiments advanced by Allen were not endorsed" by Randel and his followers, it has been pointed out by the historian of the movement, but the volume "was extensively read, being almost the only anti-Calvinistic work then in circulation."[48]

The question immediately comes to mind, why did it take the Free Will Baptists twenty years to reprint a volume they had considered to be so important in 1784? There may be at least three possible reasons for this remarkable delay. First, there is some evidence to suggest that the early Free Will Baptist demand for *Two Mites* may have been met by the then available supply of the 1781 Halifax edition. There was little need in the 1780s for hundreds of copies; scores would do and scores must have been readily available in the Nova Scotia capital. Not every Free Will Baptist either wanted or would benefit from *Two Mites;* some of the leaders, including Randel, however, did and would.

Second, Alline's "peculiar doctrines were more fully expressed" in the seventy-four page pamphlet *The Anti-Traditionalist,* first published in Halifax in 1783. *The Anti-Traditionalist* highlighted the major themes to be found in *Two Mites* but did so in a "far more rhetorical and extravagant" fashion and in a style which obviously had far more popular appeal.[49] And in the late 1780s the *Anti-Traditionalist* could be easily purchased, in reasonable numbers, from A. Henry in Halifax. *The Anti-Traditionalist,* it should be noted, was apparently republished by the Free Will Baptists in 1797, seven years before *Two Mites.* This printing schedule may reveal a great deal about the perceived significance of Alline's two pamphlets and may suggest that *The Anti-Traditionalist* was actually held in higher esteem. Such a conclusion flies in the face of all nineteenth and twentieth scholarship but nevertheless demands serious consideration.

The third possible reason for the delay in the publication of *Two Mites* was the fact that Alline's "Free Will" theology was available in a far more popular and understandable level in his *Hymns and Spiritual Songs*, first published, it will be recalled, in 1786. Publishing was an expensive business in the 1780s and the cost of producing the 340-page *Two Mites* might have discouraged the Free Will Baptist leaders who had little access to ready cash; these men even had problems feeding their families during these years. And they found it difficult to persuade "subscribers" to commit themselves to the venture. Without this funding no publisher was willing to gamble his business against such overwhelming financial and common-sense odds. There might have been a demand, beyond the "subscribers" for a hymn book, or a seventy-four page pamphlet, or even one of Alline's sermons, such as *A Sermon Preached on the 19th of February 1783 at Fort Midway*, which was reprinted under a new title, *A Gospel Call*, in Massachusetts in 1795 and again in New Hampshire in 1797. But how much demand was there for a very long, opaque, convoluted "Gingle of ... words" and "Dreadful jargon" as one especially acerbic critic described *Two Mites*?[50] It is interesting to note that *Two Mites* was never republished after 1804.

Though it may still be unclear why there was a twenty-year delay in the reprinting of *Two Mites*, it is clear that Randel was greatly influenced by its contents and also by the ideas to be found in Alline's other writings and in his hymns. In late 1783 and early 1784, Randel was desperately looking for something like Alline's theological writing in order to deal with the increasingly virulent counterattacks of his Calvinist critics and also to provide his Free Will Baptist movement with some kind of articulated ideological framework. Moreover, Randel, on a more personal level, needed some kind of intellectual justification for his Free Will commitment. But Randel and his followers needed more than this. They found in Alline a dynamic "New Light" pietism and mysticism and language which linked their movement to a Whitefieldian past and also to a nineteenth-century evangelical outlook with its special emphasis on individualism, optimism, and sense of mission. Alline was therefore a key link in the chain connecting orthodox eighteenth century evangelical thought and action with an important component of "New England Folk Religion."

Randel and his immediate successor, John Buzzell, underplayed Alline's contribution to the Free Will Baptists. Buzzell, in particular, concerned about emphasizing the American nature of the movement and Randel's formative role in it, did everything he could to ensure that Alline's influence would be regarded as of little or no consequence. In fact, in his *Life of the Elder Benjamin Randel Principally Taken From Documents Written by Himself,* Alline is not mentioned once in the text. It is as though the Falmouth preacher had never lived. However, in the official history of the Free Will Baptists, published in 1862, the Reverend I.D. Stewart, using primary documents, does devote one fifteen-line paragraph to Alline and why his *Two Mites* was important for the Free Will Baptists at a critical juncture in their early history.

IV

Only three twentieth-century scholars have examined in any detail and with any sensitivity Alline's influence on the Free Will Baptists. In 1948, the American Society of Church History published *The Great Awakening in Nova Scotia in 1776-1809,* which had been Maurice W. Armstrong's Harvard Divinity School doctoral Ph.D. thesis. For Armstrong, Alline's greatest influence on the Free Will Baptists was in the area of "Hymns and Spiritual Songs." They helped, he argued, to fuel the Second Great Awakening in New England. "From a literary point of view," he argued, "the *Hymns* are mostly doggerel." But they were "far superior to many of the crude camp-meeting hymns of the later revivals, and are a considerable improvement over much of the psalmody in use at that time in the Congregational churches." "The real significance of the hymns," Armstrong added, "lies not in their form, but in the fact that these words were the actual language of thousands of frontiersmen in that day and for thirty years afterward, and that they literally express the deepest concern of these people, both for themselves and for their families." Armstrong then concluded his

discussion by picking at random, for the sake of example, two verses
from Alline's *Hymns.*

> When I was trembling on the brink
> Of death and long despair,
> Ling'ring and fearing soon to sink,
> The Jesus did appear

> He gave my soul a heavenly peace,
> And gave me strength divine;
> He made my cutting anguish cease,
> And said that he was mine.[51]

In his sections entitled "Theological Works and Sermons" and
"Alline's Mystical Theology," Armstrong seems satisfied with reas-
serting Stewart's argument. But instead of a fifteen-line paragraph,
Armstrong is satisfied with part of one sentence, which he quotes. *Two
Mites*, for Armstrong and for Stewart was "extensively read, being
almost the only anti-Calvinist work then in circulation."[52] There is no
further discussion of the matter in Armstrong's suggestive, sensitive,
and ground-breaking study–a book which has never received the
scholarly attention and praise it certainly deserves.

Then in 1957, Norman A. Baxter's *History of The Freewill Baptists:
A Study in New England Separatism* was published. This is a terse,
understated, straightforward, narrative history which sympathetically
deals with the Free Will Baptist "revolt against Calvinism." In his second chapter entitled "The Stabilizing Period 1780–1827," Baxter first
mentions Alline. And it is noteworthy that his discussion of the
Alline–Randel connection is not informed in any way by the work of
Maurice Armstrong. Baxter, as has already been pointed out, re-
marked, concerning the 1780–1827 period, on the "startling ... paucity" of indigenous Free Will Baptist theology.[53] Baxter merely asserts
the importance of *Two Mites* and then contends that Randel "probably
... read it at an early date since it was one of the few anti-Calvinist
writings of the period and because Alline died in New Hampshire in

1784." Baxter then contends that it is to "be assumed" that Randel "was in sympathy with Alline's freedom of the will." Three separate sentences from *Two Mites* are referred to to support this statement.[54]

Baxter also discusses in one paragraph Randel's *Sermon, delivered at Farmington, New Hampshire, February 27, 1803, at the interment of Murmoth Fortune Herrick, son of Hallibut and Sally Herrick.* The sermon was probably published in 1803 or 1804 – a few years before Randel's death in 1808. "The key to the sermon," according to Baxter, "is in the one sentence, 'not one of all Adam's posterity will ever be eventually miserable because they fell in him ... there is no text of Scripture which says that any man shall be damned merely for Adam's Sin.'"[55] There is no explication of the text and no attempt made to squeeze meaning from it or to link parts of it to Alline's work. Baxter is satisfied with concluding that "Randel did not touch on the matter of the safety of the soul on this occasion, but he did emphasize the universality of the call of Christ and that He died for all men."[56]

How does Baxter account for what he refers to as "this rather amazing lack of theological discussion?" He has three reasons. First, he is certain that because the Free Will Baptists "were distinctly representative of the sect type of Christianity," they were preoccupied with "an overwhelming emphasis upon Christian life rather than upon doctrines and creeds." Second, because "the majority of early Freewill Baptist preachers were agreed on the major points of their distinctive tenets," they saw little need for "careful doctrinal exegesis." The third reason was "the humility of the early leaders" who "were unwilling to enter into arguments that would invariably generate more heat than light."[57]

Baxter's reasons are not, in any way, persuasive ones. They seem to reflect a superficial view of the evangelical sectarian mind and of New England reality. Sectarian leaders, it may be argued, suffered from a "rage to scribble *hubris*" and were always eager to debate the fine points of theology. But if they already had a spokesman, whose work was always being reprinted, perhaps they felt little need to involve themselves directly in the literary fray. This must, at least, be considered as a possible explanation – despite the siren call of Yankee chauvinism.

Stephen Marini, however, resisted this call in his finely crafted 1975 doctoral dissertation, done, as had been Armstrong's, at the Harvard Divinity School. This thesis, in much revised form, was published in 1982 as *Radical Sects in Revolutionary New England.* Marini devotes almost eighteen pages of his thesis and some eleven pages of his book to the Alline-Randel connection and his cogent and lucid analysis of evolving Free Will Baptist theology is studded with penetrating insights. Marini discusses, in a sensitive manner, and at some length, the way in which Alline's *Hymns* became the cutting edge of Free Will Baptist popular religion. Yet there is one telling error of fact in Marini's treatment of Alline's influence on the Free Will Baptists. According to Marini, in "1784 the Quarterly Meeting had been visited by Henry Alline" who had "deeply impressed Benjamin Randel by his spirituality and by the power of his theology."[58] At this meeting, Marini maintains, "Alline distributed copies of his 1781 treatise, *Two Mites ...* " Obviously, a dead Alline could not have attended the March 1784 quarterly meeting. Had he lived and had he attended the meeting, there is every reason to conclude that he would have transformed the movement and pushed it, by his powerful charismatic presence, into a radically different direction.

Marini stresses that Randel "apparently continued to use *Two Mites* as his personal theological handbook," for his "sermons and letters consistently followed Alline's formulations." And when in 1804 *Two Mites* was finally reprinted by Randel, he "deleted only Alline's argument in favor of infant baptism." "Otherwise," Randel left the new edition "intact, despite twenty years of close scrutiny."[59]

Randel's one extant sermon, *Sermon at the Interment of Murmoth Fortune,* is, as far as Marini is concerned, an almost word-for-word restatement of key sections of Alline's *Two Mites.* For example, for Randel, "The breath or nature of God is the life of the soul and body and soul must be created before the breath was breathed into Adam." All mankind were and are "seminally" present in paradise and "Adam was then really the whole Family, and the whole Family was really Adam."[60]

Mankind, like Adam and Eve, possessed what Alline had called the "power of Freewill." "Adam was invested with all that free-will and power of choice" Alline had argued, but "the whole world, body and soul, stood in him." By freely turning against God – by lusting after "another object, exclusive of his creator," mankind had "lost his life of union" with the Almighty. Man now became part of what Alline called the "animal world." Randel described humanity falling "into a state of guilt and condemnation. They broke the law of innocence, and were seminally exposed to everlasting ruin and destruction, and would have eternally sunk, for aught man or angels could have done."[61]

Because of their sin, all mankind was rushing inexorably towards eternal damnation – existing at an infinite distance away from the "Holy Presence." But God sent Christ to provide the spiritual means – "his interposing hand" – to stop this drift to black oblivion. It was, according to Randel, "Unmerited, self-moved, spontaneous love, immediately broke forth in pursuit of the rebel! ... God immediately appeared in the character of a Mediator! a Jesus! a Saviour." Carefully following every zigzag in Alline's theology, Randel declared that all time was telescoped into the "Eternal Now" and that Christ died for all at the precise moment Adam sinned. If all mankind had "been seminally" present when Adam sinned, Randel asked, "where were we when the blessed remedy appeared?" "Were we not in his loins?" "Surely we were not extracted from his loins." Randel continued, "and as the curse fell on us in his loins, surely when the glorious blessed Jesus appeared to him and the soul vanishing promise was made to him, 'the seed of the woman shall bruise the serpent's head,' we were also in his loins."[62] Marini correctly points out that:

This creation and fall episode was crucial to Free-will theology, because it replaced Calvinism's doctrine of Divine predestinating decrees "from before the foundation of the world," with an equally universal doctrine of Divine willfulness for human freedom despite original sin. The fundamental tenet of freedom of the will was worked into the creation story to show that the essence of the soul was its ability to obey or disobey God's laws, and that its destiny rested on the exercise of that ability.[63]

For Alline and for Randel the "decisive event of human history was the incarnation of Christ in the man Jesus." Christ had lived and died, not as Alline had put it, "to appease vindictive wrath, or satisfy any incensed justice in the Deity." Rather Christ's atonement was a manifestation of holy love, mercy, and grace. God wished everyone to recapture the essence of their original "Primordial union with God."[64]

As might have been expected Randel, like Alline, was fascinated by "the morphology of conversion." For Randel, "the rational powers and faculties of the soul" were completely free to relate and to respond to "the operations of the spirit of God." Conviction by the Holy Spirit was followed by repentence and then "the light, life, and love breaks into the soul, subdues the fear, removes the guilt and condemnation, takes out the state of sin, brings the soul to liberty of the sons of God, and the spirit of adoption enables him to cry Abba Father: he claims kindred with Heaven, and goes on his way rejoicing." Thus the "power of God" gets "such possession of the soul, that it is constrained to fall down, and yield up all."[65]

In experiencing the "New Birth," a person "converted to God," Randel explained, had "his sins ... all blotted out, though they were ever so great and multiplied ... yet they are all done away, and all forgiven, and will never be remembered any more. When once he has been forgiven, he will never come into condemnation for what is past." Yet there was the ever present danger of "backsliding." Randel went beyond Alline in trying to deal effectively with this thorny problem but his solution seemed to contain a major contradiction and flaw:

A soul converted and made free from condemnation for all past sins, if ever he comes into condemnation again, it must be for sin committed again, by his own voluntary consent, through his not giving heed to the divine teaching of the blessed spirit, which leadeth into all truth. For the grace of God which he has received is sufficient to keep him from falling, and to make him an overcomer, if he doth watch and pray, and continue in the way of well doing; and if he doth not, it will be his own fault – God's throne will be clear – the soul will have none to blame, neither men nor devils, but himself.[66]

If in Eden all sinned and all were redeemed, and if the "New Birth" was the means by which the "corporeal body" became "spiritual," and if the Holy Spirit did its work, how could anyone backslide permanently?

How could anyone fall "into condemnation" again? Consistency and systematic theological thinking obviously were not essential when people like Randel confronted the very real threat of "antinomianism" as well as backsliding.

Alline's theological writing obviously significantly affected all of Randel's religious thinking and provided him with the words and concepts which in turn profoundly influenced the Free Will Baptist movement. Moreover, Alline's *Hymns and Spiritual Songs* directly influenced ordinary rank-and-file Free Will Baptists. It is of some consequence, I think, that Alline's *Hymns and Spiritual Songs* was divided into five equal sections which blended together to produce a musical and popular "history of redemption." The first section was entitled "Chiefly consisting of man's fallen state," the second, "gospel invitations and a free salvation," the third, "the New Birth and the knowledge and joys of that glorious work," the fourth, "the joys and trials of the soul," and the fifth "consisting chiefly of infinite wonders, transporting views, and Christian triumphs." There was, Marini argues, a "hymnic proclivity" not only in the early Free Will Baptist movement but also among the Shakers, the Universalists, and almost every evangelical group. "A flourishing Evangelical style in both lyrics and music," permeated popular religion during the so-called "golden age" of "New England hymnody from 1775 to 1815."[67]

It has been noted that the Free Will Baptists were the last "sect" to publish their own hymnal – John Buzzell's *Psalms, Hymns and Sacred Songs* in 1823. "It is likely" he argues "that Alline's hymnal in these several editions (1786, 1795, 1797, 1802) served as the main song-book for Free-will Baptists before Buzzell's."[68] The popularity of Alline is further confirmed in Buzzell's collection; there were more of his hymns included than any other author except Isaac Watts. Alline obviously set the tone and shape of the content of Free Will hymnody until well into the nineteenth century. Even though he did not write the following "submission to Christ," Alline could have done. And this is the case with respect to almost all of the indigeneous New England hymns included by Buzzell. At this level of popular religion, Alline's influence was also both deep and widespread:

O Jesus, my saviour, to thee I submit
With joy and thanksgiving fall down at thy feet;
In sacrifice offer my soul flesh and blood,
Thou art my redeemer, my Lord, and my God.
I love thee, I love thee, I love thee, my love;
I love thee, my Saviour, I love thee my dove;
I love thee, I love thee, and that thou dost know;
But how much I love thee I never shall show.

All human expressions are empty and vain,
They cannot unriddle this heavenly flame;
I'm sure if the tongue of an angel were mine,
I could not this mystery completely define.

I'm happy, I'm happy, O wond'rous account!
My days are immortal, I stand on the Mount;
I gaze on my treasure, and long to be there,
With Jesus and angels my kindred so dear.

O who's like my Jesus? He's Salem's bright king!
He smiles and he loves me, and learns me to sing;
I'll praise him, I'll praise him, with notes loud and shrill,
While rivers of pleasure my spirit doth fill.[69]

Years earlier Alline had captured a similar theme in an evocative and memorable hymn entitled "The great love of Christ display'd in his death."

As near to Calvary I pass
Me thin[k]s I see a bloody cross,
Where a poor victim hangs.
His flesh with ragged irons tore,
His limbs all dress'd with purple gore,
Gasping in dying pangs.

Supriz'd the spectacle to see,
I ask'd who can this victim be,

> In such exquisite pain?
> I'll join to raise immortal strains,
> All ravish'd with delight.[70]

In a superb overview of the importance of hymnody for various New England "Folk Religions," Marini contends that the popular music created "preserved the major stylistic characteristics of Evangelical sacred song yet employed that style toward distinctly sectarian purposes." For him

the sects used the sensuous imagery, subjectivism, and Biblical paraphrase of Evangelical hymnody to create songs for virtually every event and activity of their religious lifestyles. The Evangelical hymn became an indispensable medium for sectarian self-expression and self-reflection. Through hymns, sectarian congregrations shared collective experiences and individuals articulated their faith. Hymn-writing in the sects had begun as a spontaneous mode of ordering the disarray of intense, even ecstatic, worship. But by 1815 the composition of sacred poetry had become a mental habit of sectarians lay and ordained, and in the publication of formal hymnals the folk religions promulgated detailed symbolization of all aspects of their identity and experience.[71]

For Marini, "Hymnody gave each sect a medium through which to render its distinctive beliefs, practices, and institutions into objective symbolic form." The actual medium "was part of the Evangelical heritage shared by all the sects, and the folk religions did not stray far from the poetic style of the Evangelical hymnists."

Sectarian hymns were for the most part derivative and imitative; the sects did not contribute anything to poetic art by their hymns. Their creativity lay in giving the hymn new content, based on their distinctive religiousness. As that religiousness developed clear-cut social forms and theological claims, the sects came to possess unique vocabularies and characteristic modes of reflection. It was these vocabularies and intellectual styles, expressive of sectarian spirituality, social design and theology, that filled the Evangelical lyric with enough new content to create a distinctly sectarian hymnody.[72]

By 1815, the distinctive Free Baptist hymnody and theology, together with a certain preaching style, all greatly influenced by Alline, it may be argued, had evolved. His neo-Whitefieldian "subjectivity and emotionalism,"[73] seemed to infuse all Free Will sacred language – as did his emphasis on the "Edenic experience," "Free Will," the "Incarnation," the "New Birth," the fusing of divine love into human action, Christian community, and the imminent return of Christ and the return to Paradise.

V

As the nineteenth century unfolded, the Free Will Baptists of northern New England found themselves torn apart by bitter sectarian centrifugal differences and by the powerful forces of alientation which were sweeping through the region. By mid century Randel's movement had been pushed to the extreme periphery of the region's religious culture. But in neighbouring New Brunswick and Nova Scotia the Free Will Baptist situation was somewhat different.

It should not be forgotten that in 1871 out of a total New Brunswick population of 285, 594 (33.6 percent of which was Roman Catholic) there were 42,729 "Calvinist Baptists – 15 percent of the population and 25,861 Free Will Baptists – 9.8 percent of the total population. Four years after Confederation, therefore, one out of every four New Brunswickers was a Baptist adherent. In Nova Scotia in 1871, out of a total population of 387,000 (26.5 percent of the population was Roman Catholic), there were only 19,032 Free Will Baptists (4.9 percent of the total population) and 54,263 Calvinist Baptists (14.0 percent of the total population.) Thus, one in five Nova Scotians was a Baptist.[74]

What this data suggests to me is that Henry Alline and his disciples – disciples in New England and New Brunswick and Nova Scotia – significantly affected the religious shape of the region not only in the Revolutionary period but throughout the nineteenth century. A decade ago I was quite wrong to suggest implicitly that Alline's premature death virtually marked the end of his great influence on people and events and rescued him from embarrassment, oblivion, and madness. My recent work on Alline's impact on post Revolutionary New England and Nova Scotia-New Brunswick suggests something quite different. It seems clear to me that he injected into Maritime Baptist religious culture a special mystical and pietistic quality and, moreoever, that he imposed on the region's evangelical tradition what has been referred to as the "neo-Whitefieldian paradigm."[75]

There were two distinct ways in which the Alline-neo-Whitefieldian evangelical tradition directly impinged upon Maritime popular religion in the late eighteenth and nineteenth centuries. First, most of Alline's early Nova Scotia disciples, men like Harris Harding, Thomas Handley Chipman, James and Edward Manning, Joseph Dimock, and Theodore Seth Harding, became leaders of the Calvinist Baptists. Though these men may have rejected Alline's anti-Calvinism and his belief that adult baptism was a "non-essential," they, nevertheless, enthusiastically endorsed his "neo-Whitefieldian paradigm" and regarded Alline as the "Apostle of Nova Scotia." Second, and this point must be emphasized, Alline exerted a noteworthy influence on the New England Free Will Baptists at a critical juncture in their historical development. With his *Two Mites* and *The Anti-Traditionalist*, Alline provided Benjamin Randel's Free Will Baptists with the theological underpinnings they so desperately needed. And, moreover, his amazingly popular *Hymns and Spiritual Songs*, became what has been called "the indispensible medium for sectarian self-expression and self-reflection."[76] Alline's *Hymns* articulated the essential Christian message in language ordinary folk could understand and could resonate with; they were "composed of those religious statements" which probably "represented the common denominator of plain-folk religious belief" and they captured the simple essence of their faith.[77] Repetition, the use of striking phrases, and the creative linking of lyrics to popular folk tunes, drilled into the inner consciousness of those who sang the *Hymns and Spiritual Songs* unforgettable experiences and the bold, unadorned rhetoric of belief.

In the early nineteenth century, a few Free Will Baptist missionaries from New England, in an ironic twist to a fascinating symbiotic relationship, came to Nova Scotia preaching, what to many native inhabitants, was Alline's gospel. As might have been expected, these Free Will Baptist missionaries, disciples of Alline, would be vociferously attacked by Calvinist Baptists, disciples too of Alline. These latter Baptists, who by the 1840s would become the Maritime mainstream, had accepted Alline's neo-Whitefieldian evangelicalism while rejecting what they termed his "doctrinal errors."[78] Thus, directly and indirectly, and this point must be underscored, Henry Alline, though never a Baptist, probably exerted more influence than any other single individual on the Baptists of New Brunswick and Nova Scotia. Moreoever, Alline significantly affected the Free Will Baptists of New England at the zenith of their influence. What Nova Scotian or Canadian, for that matter, since Alline's time can match, within the context of Canadian-American relations, the Falmouth preacher's truly remarkable accomplishment?

3

Alline, Maritime New Lights, and Baptists

Some seventy-five years after Alline's death in New Hampshire, an especially acerbic Presbyterian critic was disturbed at the continuing influence being exerted throughout western Nova Scotia by Alline. "He is spoken of as an eminent minister of the gospel," it was sadly reported in 1859, by thousands who were still convinced that he had done "more good by his labours than any minister that ever lived in Nova Scotia."[1] Most of these Nova Scotians, of course, had never met Alline face-to-face, but their positive view of the Falmouth preacher had been largely shaped by an oral culture – a culture which helped them to reconstruct a certain awareness of a distant past. These Nova Scotians saw Alline through the eyes of those of their neighbours who had actually seen and heard the "Whitefield of Nova Scotia." As late as 1856, for example, a ninety-three year old Mrs. Fox, a daughter of one of Alline's early converts – Benjamin Cleaveland, the Horton hymn-writer – still vividly remembered listening to her first Christian sermon – one preached by Alline in 1780. The sermon, she once observed, "made a deep impression on her mind;" seventy-six years after the event she still recalled Alline's text, "John XII:35." It was observed that

Mrs. Fox says she never heard Mr. Alline preach but it warmed her heart; and she heard him very often. She used frequently to travel several miles to hear him; and never heard him without there being something fresh and new in his discourses.[2]

Mrs. Fox, moreover, could still describe Alline as a man of "middling size; straight, and very thin; of light complexion, with light curly hair, and blue eyes, with a solemn expression" and his dress was "neat but plain." All of his conversation, she stressed, was "very spiritual" and Alline "would not converse about the world at all, except as urged by necessity." He "was mighty in prayer" she maintained and "was a good singer, and loved singing."[3]

Mrs. Fox and other Nova Scotians who had known Alline could only endorse with enthusiasm and conviction the last line of the inscription chiseled into his New Hampshire tombstone:

> He was a burning and shining light and was
> justly esteemed the Apostle of Nova Scotia.[4]

Despite the fact that Alline did not always preach what one Nova Scotian described in July 1784 as *"right sound doctrine,"*[5] he was, nevertheless, widely perceived in his lifetime and afterwards as a man "sent of God" who promoted a remarkable "Work of God."[6] Amos Hilton, one of Alline's most influential Yarmouth converts, expressed in 1782 what he must have realized was a widespread view concerning Alline's so-called "heretical views." When pressed by the Reverend Jonathan Scott, Alline's major Congregational Church critic, on why he could accept a gospel in which "all the Revelation of God's Word is overthrown," Hilton simply replied 'It was no Matter of any great Consequence to him what a Man's Principles were, if he was but earnest in promoting a good Work.'[7] In other words, Hilton was arguing that it was not really important what a preacher's theology actually was. What was important was whether he was truly an instrument of the Holy Spirit and his preaching moved people to experience the New Light "New Birth."

I

The essentials at least of Alline's New Light message, especially in its Nova Scotia context, contained the distinctive elements of the "radical evangelical" tradition.[8] And Marini correctly locates Alline at the heart of this Whitefieldian New Light framework. But there was also, of course, as has already been noted, an important heterodox element in the volatile mixture making up Alline's theology. And many of Alline's contemporaries were aware of the potentially explosive nature of his highly mystical theology. In a particularly discerning critique, the Reverend Mathew Richey pointed out that the Falmouth preacher's theology was a strange mixture of undigested, often conflicting, points of view. According to Richey:

They were fragments of different systems – without coherence, and without any mutual relation or dependence. With the strong assertion of man's freedom as a moral agent, he connected the doctrine of the final perseverance of the saints. He allegorized to such excess the plainest narratives and announcements of Scriptures, that the obvious and unsophisticated import of the words of inspiration was often entirely lost amidst the reveries of mysticism.[9]

Not all of Alline's followers, however, would be as concerned as he was with neutralizing the antinomian potential of the "perseverance of the saints" by stressing the importance of living the "good Christian life." But the vast majority would be content to remain traditional Allinite "New Lights," orthodox yet mystical, obsessed as was their charismatic leader with the "rapture" and "ecstasy" of the "New Birth." Such men and women, not surprisingly, sang with enthusiasm the "New Light" hymn and made it their own unique testimony:

Come all who are New-lights indeed,
Who are from sin and bondage freed;
From Egypts land we've took our flight,
For God has given us a New-light.

Long time we with the wicked trod,
And madly ran the sinful road;
Against the gospel we did fight,
Scar'd at the name of a New-light.

At length the Lord in mercy call'd,
And gave us strength to give up all;
He gave us grace to choose aright,
A portion with despised New-lights.

Though by the world we are disdain'd,
And have our names cast out by men;
Yet Christ our captain for us fights,
Nor death, nor hell, can hurt New Lights.

I know not any sect or part,
But such as are New-Lights in heart;
If in Christ Jesus you delight,
I can pronounce you a New-Light.

For since in Christ we all are one,
My soul would fain let strife alone;
No prejudice can any bear,
Nor wrath, in those who New-lights are.

Thus guarded by the Lord we stand,
Safe in the hollow of his hand;
Nor do we scorn the New-Light's name,
The saints are all New-Lights, Amen.

Amen, Amen, so let it be,
Glory to God, this light we see;
New light from Christ to us is given,
New light will be our light in heaven.[10]

Most Nova Scotians, during and after Alline's lifetime were not overly concerned with his so-called "heretical views," realizing the centrality of the New Light "radical evangelicalism" in his Christian message. A perceptive critic of the religious life of Nova Scotia and certainly a person who was not a New Light enthusiast, Simeon Perkins, the Liverpool merchant and civic leader, observed on Sunday, February 11, 1783

Mr. Alline made a long Speech, Very Sensible, Advising all Sorts of People to a Religious Life, and gave many directions for their outward walk. This is a wonderful day and Evening. Never did I behold such an Appearance of the Spirit of God moving upon the people since the time of the Great Religious Stir in New England many years ago.[11]

Perkins, it is clear, carefully fitted Alline into the orthodox New Light framework. Most other Nova Scotians of the time, the evidence suggests, would have done precisely the same thing despite all the evidence which could have pushed them toward a radically different interpretation.

Alline had intuitively realized that most Nova Scotians, during the American Revolution, were acutely troubled and disoriented and were desperately searching for some meaning in life and for meaningful relationships. And Alline saw that the "New Birth" provided both. It is interesting, and I deliberately re-emphasize the point, that Alline made extraordinary use of sexual imagery in order to convey something of the rich emotional texture of conversion. Conversion, for him, was perceived as a spiritual climax, the consummation of an intense love-hate relationship which seemed to be the essence of conviction. For Alline, conversion was, as he often graphically put it "being married to Christ." And it was a "marriage" to the "Heavenly Charmer" which would give meaning and order to all other relationships.[12]

Those Nova Scotians who were converted under his preaching or by his disciples, wished to replicate all aspects of Alline's own transforming religious experience. They too wished to see Paradise; they too wished to "taste but one glimmering ray" of the "Eternal Now."[13] And they yearned for Alline's Christ to ravish them to make them one with him. They sought the mountain peak of religious ecstacy but naively underestimated how difficult it would be for them to remain there. Many would tumble to the depths of despair soon after Alline's death. But most would never forget that magic New Light moment when they, like Henry Alline, had experienced Jesus Christ and had become part of his pristine spirituality and perfectability. They had reached out and Christ had touched them. They were certain that it could happen again – and it did, only a few years after Alline's death – as periodic revivals became a distinguishing feature of Nova Scotia's religious culture.

Contemporary critics of Alline and of the New Lights, however, perceived the evangelical ethos in a radically different manner. The Reverend Jacob Bailey, for example, the Anglican priest and Loyalist writer, hated them with a finely tuned passion. In 1789, he penned a "Verse Against the New Lights" which, though distorted by his despair and lack of any empathy for religious enthusiasm, nevertheless conveyed some critical truths about his New Light enemies. And Bailey's verse does provide the other side to the New Light coin:

> Behold the gifted teacher rise
> And roll to heaven his half-shut eyes;
> In every feature of his face

See stiffness sanctity and grace
Like whipping post erect he stands
Then with a slow and gentle voice
Begins to make a languid noise
Strives with a thousand airs to move
To melt and thaw your hearts to love
But when he fails by soft'ning arts
To mollify your frozen hearts
Observe him spring with eager jump
And on the table fiercely thump
With double fist he beats the air
Pours out his soul in wrathful prayer
Then seized with furious agitation
Screams forth a frightful exhortation
And with a sharp and hideous yell
Sends all your carnal folks to hell
Now to excite your fear and wonder
Tries the big jarring voice of thunder
Like wounded serpent in the vale
He writhes his body and his tail
Strives by each motion to express
The Agonies of deep distress
Then groans and scolds and roars aloud
Till dread and frenzy fire the crowd
The madness spreads with rapid power
Confusion reigns and wild uproar
A concert grand of joyful tones
Mingled with sighs and rueful moans
Some heaven extol with rapturous air
While others rave in black despair
A blended group of different voices
Confound and stun us with their noises
Thus in some far and lonely site
Amidst the deepest glooms of night

> Where roll the slow and sullen floods
> O'er hung with rocks and dusky woods
> I've heard the wolves terrific howl
> The doleful music of the owl
> The frogs in hoarser murmurs croak
> While from the top of some tall oak
> With notes more piercing soft and shrill
> Resounds the spritely whip-poor-will
> These give the ears of wonderous greeting
> Not much unlike a pious meeting
> Here blue-eyed Jenny plays her part
> Inured to every saint-like art
> She works and heaves from head to heel
> With pangs of puritanic zeal
> Now in a fit of deep distress
> The holy maid turns prophetess
> And to her light and knowledge brings
> A multitude of secret things
> And as Enthusiasm advances
> Falls into ecstasies and trances
> Her self with decency resigns
> To these impulses and inclines
> On Jemmy Trim a favourite youth
> A chosen vessel of the truth
> Who as she sinks into his arms
> Feels through his veins her powerful charms
> Grown warm with throbs of strong devotion
> He finds his blood in high commotion
> And fired with love of this dear sister
> Is now unable to resist her[14]

There were, without question, some Jemmy Trims in Nova Scotia and some "blue-eyed" Jennys. And the critics of the New Lights would never permit their enemies to forget this.

II

Nova Scotia, especially Yankee Nova Scotia, had, in a religious sense, been assiduously cultivated by Alline and his disciples throughout the Revolutionary years. Though most observers agreed with Alline that by early 1781 the "Great Awakening" had lost much of its earlier momentum in the Yankee heartland of the colony, he and Thomas Handley Chipman and Joseph Bailey and John Payzant continued to preach the evangelical gospel in the more peripheral regions such as the St John River Valley and the South Shore. After Alline's death, these three disciples did not stop preaching, of course. But because each was now married, with family responsibilities, and lacking Alline's example and inspiration, they began to limit somewhat their itinerating. But a Methodist counteroffensive, begun in 1785 by Freeborn Garrettson, a very gifted preacher from Maryland, forced them to defend the Allinite New Light legacy and in the process they helped in bringing about the transformation of Alline's disorganized sect into the Baptist Church.

It should be kept in mind that during the years immediately following the end of the American War of Independence, much of Nova Scotia was experiencing yet another profound, and for many disconcerting, collective sense of acute disorientation and confusion.[15] As was the case in neighbouring northern New England, hundreds of "common people were cut loose from all sorts of traditional bonds and found themselves freer, more independent, more unconstrained than ever before in their history."[16] The coming of over 20,000 Loyalists to peninsular Nova Scotia at the end of the Revolution accelerated a process of social disintegration already underway. The Loyalists, according to Edward Manning, had a "bad and . . . dreadful effect" on the colony and they "corrupted" societal values and made many Nova Scotians "adepts in wickedness."[17] Thus, as Gordon Wood has argued, with respect to New England – and his argument may also be applied to Nova Scotia – "Traditional structures of authority crumbled under the momentum of the Revolution, and common people increasingly discovered that they no longer had to accept the old distinctions" that had driven them into a widely-perceived subservient and vulnerable status.[18] And, as might have been expected, sometime "bizarre but emotionally satisfying ways of relating to God and others" became increasingly widespread phenomena as many Nova Scotians sought a renewed sense of "community-belonging" in order to neutralize the powerful forces of alienation then sweeping the colony. It was a period when, it has been perceptively observed, "everything was believable" and "everything could be doubted." "Radical enthusiasts and visionaries," regarding themselves as the disciples of Henry Alline and as propagators of his tradition, became the "advanced guard" of the renewed "popular evangelical movement with which they shared a common hostility to orthodox authority."[19] By 1790 these New Lights, as they were spitefully referred to by their enemies, were a people in a delicate state of spiritual tension "poised like a steel spring by the contradicting forces pulling within it." There was a mystical quality; but there was also a secular one; there was a democratic bias but also an authoritarian one, a revelating emphasis and an empirical tendency, and both an obsession with individualism and a tendency towards communitarianism. For some, it seems clear, the seemingly contradictory forces within the New Lights would soon neutralize one another, producing apathy, indifference, and disenchantment. For others, a not insignificant number, the dynamic tension would result in a renewed pietism which would become a crucial link in the chain connecting Henry Alline's First Great Awakening and Nova Scotia's Second Great Awakening. But for an influential minority, known as the "New Dispensationalists" by friends and enemies alike, the state of spiritual tension brought about by the coming of the Loyalists, the Garrettsonian revival, the continuing influence of Alline's legacy and growing American sectarian influences, provided a marvellous opportunity to stretch Alline's gospel to and beyond the antinomian breakingpoint.[20]

Critically important actors in the unfolding New Light drama in Nova Scotia in the decade or so following Alline's quitting the colony were Edward and James Manning, Joseph Dimock, and Harris Harding. All of these men played key roles not only in breathing new life into the New Light movement in the late 1780s but also in encouraging and in facilitating for a time at least the growth of New Dispensationalism. Moreover, after the New Dispensationalists had spun off into a state of spiritual anarchy, they helped to undermine the new, divisive, and embarrassing sect by, among other things, channelling a New Light majority into the Calvinist Baptist Church. It seems that some of Alline's followers – even during his life-time – probably spun his New Light gospel in the direction of antinomianism. Having experienced the "ravishing of the spirit" and the "rapture of the New Birth," these men and women could not imagine how they could lose their salvation. And their confidence and certainty of redemption was such that they became increasingly indifferent to sin and to contemporary moral standards. Most of Alline's followers, of course, were not antinomians. But some were, for varying lengths of time, especially in the New Light heartland area of Cornwallis and Falmouth and in Cumberland and along the St John River valley. The most significant manifestation of New Light antinomianism probably occurred in 1791 in the Cornwallis area. At the core of the movement were to be found Harris Harding, Edward Manning and his brother James, and Joseph Dimock, as well as the influential teacher Thomas Bennett, and Lydia Randall.[21] For at least one outside observer, Freeborn Garrettson, Mrs. Randall was evidently "their head speaker"[22] and according to the Reverend John Payzant, an insider, she orchestrated in May 1791 the denunciation of "all the orders of the church."[23] As far as other contemporaries were concerned, Harris Harding was the principal actor in the so-called New Dispensation movement. The term "New Dispensation" was used by contemporaries to describe this Nova Scotian manifestation of antinomianism.

The persistent struggle with his New Dispensation enemies both exhausted and depressed Payzant who in April 1793 jumped at the opportunity to minister to the Liverpool New Light Congregational Church. Two years later, Edward Manning was ordained as the minister of the Cornwallis New Light Church. By late 1793, it seems clear, the New Dispensation movement was on the decline, especially in the Horton-Cornwallis region. The Mannings and Joseph Dimock, and

possibly Thomas Bennett, had been frightened and then appalled by
the antinomian excesses practised by some of their former associates.
Moreover, the chaos and disorder which seemed endemic to the movement appeared to threaten seriously the already fragile underpinnings
of Nova Scotia society. Short term ecstasy was one thing; permanent
confusion and disorientation was quite a different matter.[24]

It should be kept in mind that in 1791, Harding was thirty-one years
old, Joseph Dimock was twenty-four, James Manning, twenty-eight,
and his brother Edward, twenty-six. All were still unmarried and, the
evidence suggests, physically attractive, full of energy, and convinced that they were divinely ordained instruments for the spiritual
transformation not only of Nova Scotia and New Brunswick but also
of northern New England. Their preoccupation with itinerating helped
considerably not only to extend the territorial boundaries of the 1789
"Reformation" but also to encourage the extraordinary growth of both
the New Dispensation movement and what may be regarded as an
energized New Light pietism. But by late 1793, the evidence suggests
that the Mannings and Joseph Dimock had declared their independence of the increasingly manichaen-oriented New Dispensationalists
and had chosen, instead, to be at the cutting edge of a renewed and far
more orthodox pietism. In other words, these men, reacting violently
against antinomian excesses they no longer could condone or control,
returned to the neo-Whitefieldian framework – but one which no longer
emphasized – as it had – the central importance of feelings and impressions. Harris Harding, however, continued to preach what Simeon
Perkins called "the Antinomian doctrines"[25] – and he remained a principal actor in the movement until the concluding years of the eighteenth
century. And there would be those in Nova Scotia who would argue
that he remained sympathetic to the movement until his death in 1854.
But these critics were wrong. Harding, in the nineteenth century, was
not an advocate of New Dispensationalism. Rather, he continued to
be an enthusiastic disciple of Henry Alline and what was frequently
referred to as "Allinism."[26]

After he had become the general factotum of the Nova Scotia
Baptist Church, an ardent Calvinist and a vociferous critic of New

Light enthusiasm, Edward Manning attempted to describe what he considered to be the heart of New Dispensationalism:

> Mr. Alline's lax observance of divine institutions fostered in the minds of his followers such ideas as these; that the ordinances are only circumstantials, outward matters, and mere non-essentials; that the scriptures are not the only rule of faith and practice; and that no person is under any obligation to perform any external duty until God immediately impresses the mind so to do. . . . Several began to question the propriety of having anything to do with external order or ordinances, and soon refused to commune with the church. . . . As they had no rule to go by but their fancies, which they called "the Spirit of God," great irregularities ensued.[27]

Manning, who for the remainder of his life would be embarrrassed by his close association in the 1790–2 period with the New Dispensationalists, had deftly cut to the heart of the movement's ideology. Here was a man who had played a key role in coaxing the movement into existence and who had, moreover, significantly affected its evolution. If any single person understood New Dispensationalism and its appeal, Edward Manning certainly did. As far as he was concerned, it was Alline's "lax observance of divine institutions" and his emphasis on the "Spirit of Liberty" and "individual illumination" which persuaded many of his followers to break out of the radical evangelical and New Light framework to enjoy what to many was regarded as "Quaker and Shaker" freedom. There was a deep desire to experiment, to shatter existing religious values, to reshape fundamentally evangelical individualism, and to challenge frontally community norms. With the Spirit of God within them, having experienced the intensity and the rapture of the New Birth, having been ravished by the Almighty, anything seemed possible and permissible. Their sin had been cancelled out, once and for all, by the sacrifice of Christ, and sinning, whether in the flesh or the spirit, could not distance them from their Saviour. Instead of turning towards ascetic behaviour, as Alline had preached and practised, many New Dispensationalists, driven by the "Spirit of Liberty," and in order to test the viability of their New Birth and to flaunt their spiritual *hubris* at their neighbours, committed what

Manning called "their extravagancies." Their "great irregularities" obviously served a number of interrelated purposes. They were the means whereby one could both enjoy sin and appreciate salvation – no insignificant accomplishment in any age. "Antinomian excesses," moreover, enabled men and women to express freely and creatively their innermost emotional and sexual desires and drives at a time, and in an age, when such behaviour was regarded as being sinfully aberrant.[28]

III

It would be a serious mistake, however, to suppose that all those individuals described by their critics as New Dispensationalists were in fact guilty of gross antinomian excesses. Some were, but how many it is now impossible to say. Far more, the vast majority, inspired by the "Spirit of Liberty," were satisfied with questioning existing church rules and regulations and with proposing a fundamental restructuring of religious worship. This questioning of authority as well as this actual assertion of independence was, it may be argued, a revolutionary development. Societal values were challenged directly and found disconcertingly wanting. These people, in many respects, were Allinites; they were regarded by their enemies as disciples of the Falmouth preacher and proudly perceived themselves in precisely these terms. They were carrying on Alline's traditions in a colony that had abandoned the principles undergirding the First Great Awakening.

During the second decade of the nineteenth century what were then disparagingly referred to as the "old New Lights" were still trying desperately to keep alive the essentials of Alline's gospel.[29] These men and women were not then regarded as antinomian extremists; probably most never had been. Rather, as one critic succinctly put it, they were "genuine Christian[s]." "They had," he went on, "more experiences than doctrine – more imagination than judgment – more spiritualism than spirituality – more of the ideal than the substantial."

They had no ordinances, no creed, no discipline. They paid little or nothing to support religion, either at home or abroad. To pay money for religion was with them one of the greatest abominations the sun ever shone upon. But they believed in regeneration by the Spirit, in Christ as a Saviour, and in heaven and hell. But they were not uniform, or at all agreed in what they did believe. Their religion was all feeling. Every thing in the Bible, in the Old or New Testament, was but allegorical, and was what all Christians experience. Abel was nothing but the new spiritual life working in us; and his acceptable offering humility, love and faith, the sacrifices acceptable to God.[30]

According to the Reverend David Nutter, a leading Baptist, "their notions about religion were . . . the most singular I had ever met with." Nutter was, he stressed, "exceedingly amused, not to say entertained, to hear them explain Scripture history, and Scripture characters; to notice how flexible and versatile the imagination of one can become by use and practice."[31] But despite this biting criticism, Nutter still regarded these disciples of Alline as "genuine Christian[s]."[32] They were "old New Lights" indeed and because of the challenge they posed to the burgeoning Baptist Church in Nova Scotia, they were unceremoniously pushed into a dark corner of oblivion. The New Lights were an embarrassing reminder of what so many Nova Scotia Calvinist Baptists had once been and there was a deep psychological need apparently for key Calvinist Baptist leaders to try to wipe the collective memory free of Alline's peculiar views. But in the process not only was Alline's heterodoxy excised from the Nova Scotia Calvinist Baptist mind but also much of his "radical evangelicalism." Thus, in their search for respectability and order, the Nova Scotia Baptist leadership jettisoned much of the emotionalism and evangelical spirituality which was at the heart of Alline's message. The result, in a particularly ironic twist of fate, was that the Baptists, in many respects, appropriated much of the theological perspective of eighteenth-century Calvinist Congregationalism. There is therefore, some truth in the contention that the views of Jonathan Scott were as significant an influence on evolving nineteenth-century Nova Scotia Baptist development as were those of Henry Alline. Scott's *A Brief View* had triumphed over Alline's *Two Mites* – after all.[33] Or had it? On one level, it triumphed – at the level of leadership – among men like Edward Manning, for example.

But at the grass roots level, Alline's influence continued to be of considerable importance. As Esther Clark Wright has correctly observed, too little has been written – in the existing sparse literature – about the significant "work of the laymen in maintaining the Baptist Churches." "The competency of the individual in religion" she has asserted, "make it possible to carry on without prophet, priest, or king – or even an ordained Baptist minister."[34] In many regions of Nova Scotia and New Brunswick, concerned lay people, many of whom were familiar with the Allinite traditions and its New Light manifestations, stubbornly resisted the seeming inexorable flow of the Baptist Calvinist mainstream.

If any one individual was responsible for the significant downplaying of the New Light influence in the Maritime Baptist tradition, it was Edward Manning. Reacting violently against his own New Light Free Will past, Manning did everything in his power to ensure that the New Light legacy would atrophy into dark oblivion. Manning was obviously haunted by his Allinite past and determined that the painful lesson he had learned in the 1790s would become his denomination's major ideological construct. Moreover, he accurately linked the remarkable growth of the Free Will Baptists in Nova Scotia and New Brunswick with what he called "Allinism" which he argued made people "more confounded than comforted!" Throughout the first half of the nineteenth century until his death in 1851, Manning did everything in his power to encourage his Baptist Church to define its separate identity by behaving in a radically different manner from the Allinite Free Will Baptist enthusiasts. Manning did not want to abandon his revised version of the Whitefieldian paradigm; what he wished to do was to get rid of what he regarded as New Light excesses and "extravagancy." Some might argue that this response was merely the working out of what Freud called the "narcissism of small differences." Others would argue, perhaps more persuasively, that Manning and the Baptist "ministerial elite" were overly concerned with respectability and were therefore eager to sacrifice an integral part of their rich historical tradition in order to become a respectable part of the Maritime Protestant consensus. They had overreacted quite understandably to New

Dispensationalism by exaggerating, among other things, its appeal. Moreover, they had underestimated the broadly based popular support for Henry Alline's brand of New Light radical evangelicalism that continued to undergird both the Free Will and Calvinist Baptists until, at least, later in the nineteenth century. It has been recently argued in an interesting study of the impact of the "Antinomian Challenge" on both the New Lights in Nova Scotia and the evolving Baptist Church that "Alline's Great Awakening presaged the breakdown of the old order and the emergence of another social framework." Moreover,

New Dispensationalism was a part of this "fermentation process" whereby varied elements clashed, struggled for dominance, and were altered. Changes in government policy or economic ups-and-downs touched only the exterior life. War with the United States forced Nova Scotians to readjust mentally their attitude toward their southern neighbour and consider their own "national identity." Religious crises demand changes within an individual's conscious perception of himself and the world around him. Evangelical rivalry in colonial Nova Scotia among Methodists, Baptists, New Lights and to some extent Anglicans, including the challenge of antinomianism to orthodox, traditional sects, resulted in a revolution of the mind. Reaction to Dispensation freedoms and conservative orderliness shaped within a large segment of early Nova Scotian society a sense of values and tensions which had yet to be resolved during the course of the nineteenth century. The forces at work among eighteenth century founders resulted in an experience unique to the Nova Scotia setting, and in no small measure shaped a new identity.[35]

It would be a serious distortion of the historical past to suggest either implicitly or explicitly that the Nova Scotia Baptist Church – in the post Alline period – was simply what has been described as "a negative reaction" to the "Antinomian challenge" of the early 1790s. Obviously, the sudden and, to some, remarkable growth of the Calvinist Baptist movement owed something to this defensive response. But even this response must be viewed in a larger perspective and must take into account a variety of complex forces and the roles played by a number of principal participants. One of these was Thomas Handley Chipman – an early Alline convert – who, unlike his mentor, regarded baptism by immersion as anything but a "nonessential." Soon after his conversion, Chipman had been baptized by immersion in 1779. And if any single individual in Nova Scotia in the 1780s and 1790s tried to push the New Light movement in the direction of the Baptist Church, it was Chipman – from his vantage-point at Granville. Chipman's task was made somewhat easier because he was widely known and deeply revered throughout Nova Scotia as one of Alline's closest associates. He had travelled widely with Alline; he had preached with him; he had suffered with Alline and he had shared in the Falmouth minister's spiritual ecstasy and black, morbid introspection. Chipman had been legitimized by Alline's success and friendship. He struggled long and hard to prevent the New Light mainstream from being absorbed by antinomian "New Dispensationalism." But he did more than this; after the defeat of New Dispensationalism, Chipman assiduously channelled New Light revivalism into a Calvinist Baptist organizational framework.[36]

IV

What has sometimes been referred to as Nova Scotia's "Second Great Awakening" began in the late 1790s and continued until at least 1810. At the cutting edge of the spiritual movement – the "Great Reformation" as contemporaries referred to it – were Allinite disciples like Chipman, Harris Harding, the Mannings, and Joseph Dimock. The "Awakening" seemed to begin at Horton and then it radiated in all directions – up into the St John River Valley, into Cumberland, down the Annapolis Valley to Yarmouth and into Argyle and Barrington. It was, in many respects, a Baptist revival. There was therefore a great deal of truth in Bishop Charles Inglis' report to the Society for the Propagation for the Gospel in which he warned of "the prevalence of an enthusiastic and dangerous spirit among a sect in the Province called New Lights, whose religion seems to be a strange jumble of New England independence and Behmenism. Formerly they were Pedobaptists, but by a recent illumination, they have adopted the Anabaptist scheme, by which their number has been much increased and their zeal enflamed."[37] Inglis was particularly concerned with Harris Harding's impact. According to the Bishop, intelligence from the Yarmouth area stressed that

A rage for dipping or total immersion prevails all over the western counties of the Province, and is frequently performed in a very indelicate manner before vast collections of people. Several hundreds have already been baptized, and this plunging they deem to be absolutely necessary to the conversion of their souls.[38]

Inglis also charged that the Baptist leaders were "engaged in a general plan of total revolution in religion and civil government."[39] Clearly, there was no substantiation for this charge or for Inglis' contention that the Baptist preachers were dangerously influenced by the work of Thomas Paine.

The Anglican bishop, despite some of the glaring inaccuracies in his report, nevertheless had correctly perceived the important trans-formation of many New Lights into Baptists. Concerned about the need for order and discipline, Payzant, the Mannings, and Thomas Handley Chipman met in July 1797, and agreed "to walk together in fellowship as ministers of Jesus Christ" and "to hold a yearly conference, to know our minds, and the state of the different churches standing in connection, by their delegates being sent by them."[40] In June 1798, the Conference took place at Cornwallis. According to Edward Manning's minutes:

Mr. Handly Chipman spoke concerning the nature of an Association . . . Met again at five o'clock. Discoursed largely upon the necessity of order and discipline in the churches, and continued until midnight in observing the dangerous tendency of erroneous principles and practices, and lamenting the unhappy consequences in our churches.[41]

Harris Harding requested admission to the Conference. It was pointed out that he had "deeply fallen into errors" by continuing to espouse the cause of New Dispensationalism. Harding "professed sorrow, humbly acknowledged his offences, signed a document to that effect, craved forgiveness of his brethren, and was received."[42] Sometime in 1799, the Reverend Thomas Handley Chipman visited Boston to confer with the Reverend Samuel Stillman, the minister of the First Baptist Church in Boston, about a suit brought against Enoch Towner, an ordained Nova Scotia Baptist minister, for conducting an illegal marriage. (At this time, only Church of England ministers could, officially, at least, conduct marriage ceremonies.) Chipman was also in Boston collecting ammunition for his final assault on the decaying outworks of the New Light Church. At the annual Conference held in 1800, Chipman presented "a close Baptist communion plan."[43] The Reverend John Payzant was furious. When he confronted Chipman, the Annapolis preacher replied "that Mr. Towner had been sued for Marrying and in order to defend the suit he had adopted that plan, that they might be called by some name for they were looked upon as nobody."[44] As Baptists they would have some status in the community; they could stress their link with "the Danbury Association in New England."[45] Without this link and without the name they were without power and influence. It was proposed that the Association name be changed from "Congregational and Baptist," to "The Nova Scotia Baptist Association."[46] The Mannings, Dimock, Chipman, the Hardings and Towner, Joseph Crandall, a New Brunswick preacher (but not Payzant) accepted their certificates as members of the Baptist Association. It was then agreed by the Baptist ministers present that:

As many aspersions are cast upon the churches of Christ and the ministers of the gospel, for erroneous principles, etc., the associated ministers and messengers judge it expedient that our church articles of faith and practice should be printed, and the Churches in connection should defray the expense of printing said articles, and the plan of the Association.[47]

Certain key Allinites had in 1800 become Nova Scotia Baptists. But there were some reluctant signers – including Harris Harding and

Joseph Dimock – both of whom had been very close to the New Light Allinites in the post-1784 period and both of whom remained, for a time, suspicious of Calvinism's allure and the advisability of closed-communion churches. In these churches, those New Lights who refused to be baptized by immersion, and who also resisted Church discipline, would be compelled to leave the "fellowship of believers." Alline's "non-essential," adult baptism, had become a Baptist, closed-communion, "essential." Alline's flexible New Light Church policy had been replaced by an inflexible Calvinist Baptist one.

Eventually three churches – Yarmouth, Argyle, and Chester – withdrew from the Baptist Association largely over the matter of "closed communion," and each of these churches had close ties with Harris Harding. In 1808 there were 1,248 members in the eleven Nova Scotia churches belonging to the Association. In 1809, after the withdrawal, there were only 753 in the eight closed-communion Baptist churches. Harris Harding's church had been the second largest in the Association – 250 strong as against Horton's 276. It was not until 1828 that Harding's church was reunited to the Association. In 1811 Chester rejoined and in 1837 Argyle, in somewhat different form, returned to the Baptist fold.[48]

It would be a mistake to exaggerate the influence of the six so-called patriarchs, the Mannings, Chipman, the Hardings, and Joseph Dimock in the fascinating symbiotic relationship connecting Nova Scotia's Second Great Awakening with the transformation of the New Light movement into the Baptist Church. Nor should these be under-estimated. They were not charismatic religious leaders in the Alline tradition. Nor were they organizational giants like the Reverend Timothy Dwight, who from his Yale University base, helped to orchestrate the Second Great Awakening in New England in the 1795 to 1815 period. But it may be argued that they were important links between the First and the Second Great Awakenings. They succeeded in applying the Alline paradigm of revitalization to another chronological period and to a different mix of people. It was a paradigm which stressed the central importance of the conversion experience, intense piety, ecstatic worship forms, Biblical literalism and the pure church ideal. In many respects, the human links between the two Awakenings were sensitive reflectors of the religious aspirations of the thousands of Nova Scotians to whom they diligently preached their often emotional and introspective version of the Christian gospel. American influences, direct and indirect, events in Europe, and economic and social stress in Nova Scotia may have provided the general framework in which the Second Great Awakening worked itself out. Yet without such men, no "Great Reformation" would have been possible; and without them, moreover, the "Great Reformation" would have been quite a different kind of religious movement.

According to the 1827 Nova Scotia census, the New Light Baptist counter-offensive had been amazingly successful. The total population of Nova Scotia in 1827 was estimated at 123,630. This included 28,655 Anglicans, 37,647 Presbyterians, 20,401 Roman Catholics, 19,790 Baptists, 9,408 Methodists, 2,968 Lutherans and 4,761 others. The Baptist percentage in 1827 was 16.0 percent and the Methodist 7.7 percent. By 1871, there were 73,295 Baptists, 18.9 percent of the total Nova Scotia population of 387,800 and 40,345 Methodists, 10.4 percent of the total.[49] In New Brunswick, by mid-century, the Baptists were the largest Protestant denomination. Alline's disciples, in their nineteenth-century Baptist manifestation, had indeed made remarkable numerical gains.

V

There are two other important ways in which Alline's New Light legacy affected Maritime Baptists in particular and the region's evangelical ethos in general. This New Light legacy, it may be argued, had a more lasting and more significant overall impact on the religious life of New Brunswick than that of Nova Scotia. The experience of Elder James Innis, a New Brunswick New Light Baptist preacher in Nova Scotia in 1805 is, I think, extremely illuminating in this regard. Innis was a former British soldier who had settled in New Brunswick after the American Revolution. An uneducated farmer, after his conversion he was ordained as an elder in the Horton, New Brunswick Baptist Church in 1800 by Edward Manning and Theodore Seth Harding of Cornwallis and Horton respectively. Innis kept a fascinating diary[50] in which both implicitly and explicitly he distinguished his New Brunswick New Light Allinite views from the ordered Calvinism of the two Nova Scotia patriarchs, Manning and T.S. Harding.

While visiting Nova Scotia in 1805, as an itinerant, Innis preached first in the Horton area. With Harding present, Innis "opend the meeting" with a "Song and Prayer" and then "opend my Bibil and Gave out a Teaxt." While he was preaching to what he referred to as a "house . . . full of people," a woman near him "fell at full length on the floor Crying for Marcy and Beating the flour with her hands." Others in the congregation were soon "all Rejoicing in the Lord in wonderful manner." The following day, Innis preached in the regular church service and "Reached many hearts and Brought many tears and caused a sister to Break out in praise to God." "Seven came forward and told their experiences," he observed. "Six they Received but would not receive one that was Coller [Coloured] which caused Much Contension between me and Mr. H[arding] and Church." As far as the indignant Innis was concerned, Harding was not justified in "Shut[ting] the Gates of Heaven against her." He denounced Harding as being "nothing Better then a hirling and to let the people Go free." Harding replied by telling Innis that he could "Preach" but that only the Horton minister "would Baptize." A few days later, Harding was no longer certain that Innis should even be preaching in the area. His "roving Commission" was creating divisions in the community and his preaching was triggering embarrassing emotional excesses.

News about the Harding-Innis controversy reached Edward Manning before Innis actually arrived in the Cornwallis area. According to Innis, Manning "thought that every Sheef should Bow to his Shef" but the New Brunswick preacher "told him my order was to Salute no man . . . as I was Desired by the tender Spirit of God, for he Seamed to think I ought to Go as he desired . . . but I came to Cry against the alter of Baal." "Our Conversation" Innis reported "was not like that was ingaged to the advancement of the dear Redeemer's Kingdom, for he thought himself Sumbody but I was nothing and less than Nothing."

Moreover, Manning "Blamed" Innis "for making Christians before God had made them."

The Manning-Harding negative reaction to Innis was shaped, it seems clear, by a deeply held fear of both the style and the substance of the New Brunswick preacher's message. Innis loved to encourage, what he once described, as "the Bitter Pangs of the New Birth" and he, furthermore, often underscored "the Truth" of Henry Alline's gospel. Not only did Innis evidently question the validity of Calvinism but he also questioned the role of the settled minister. Like Alline and like Manning in his early career, Innis was determined, as he put it, "to Cry against the alter of Baal" wherever the Holy Spirit directed him. And as far as Innis was concerned, his own experience and that of others he knew well, convincingly showed that true religion was of the "heart" and not of the "head." When he died in 1817, his religious views had not altered despite what he once described as the "Great Tryals and Strugles in my own mind for the Powers of darkness worked much with me."

The "Powers of darkness'" which confronted the Reverend Thomas Griffin in Saint John in 1818 were quite different from those which had assailed Innis a few years earlier. In fact, these "Powers," as far as Griffin was concerned, were those influencing the Innis-New Light tradition. Griffin was a distinguished Baptist minister from Kidderminster, England; he became minister of Germain St Baptist Church, Saint John, either in late 1817 or early in 1818. His sojourn in New Brunswick, however, was brief; by 1819, he had made his way to Philadelphia to serve a Baptist Church there.

In his correspondence with Edward Manning, Griffin emphasized his lack of sympathy and empathy for what he knew as New Brunswick New Light Baptists. English Baptist Calvinist decorum and its Nova Scotia variant was one thing. New Brunswick New Light enthusiasm was quite another. "We have a few of the new light sort amongst us," Griffin informed Manning in September 1818, "they want to feel religion – ie. something to ferment like yeast and then as flat as water – something that will set them going tho they live in neglect of watchfulness prayer and God's ordanances." Griffin then concluded

My ideas of religion are of a more rational and permanent kind, the enjoyment
of God must be in duty (tho not for it) and always stands connected with
holiness; not an in and out noisy irreverent profession, but an humble daily
walk with God.[51]

Early in November, Griffin developed further his anti-New Brunswick
New Light critique. "It is grievous to see people taken with any person
who comes," he sadly reported to Manning "and evince the want of
stability and judgment in this manner, if a man take a text and totally
forget it, speak in the most improper manner as to pronunciation, snuff
at the nose as if nothing shd be lost, and dance with feet like a weaver
in his loom, contradict himself often, and speak so as you could not
discuss whether he be an Arminian or not this will do." "You must
not suppose our people are generally of the sort described," Griffin
added, "but there is enough to make a Minister uneasy: but many things
shall be omitted, or you will think me of a murmuring disposition. I
cannot lick peoples feet, I cannot disguise my sentiments. . . . In short
I am too much of John Bull."[52]

In that last sentence, Griffin cogently summarized his basic difference
with those so-called New Lights in his congregation. And he knew,
moreover, that Manning enthusiastically endorsed his position. Manning too, refused to "lick peoples feet"; Manning, too, was attached to
a structured Baptist Calvinist position in theology as well as in church
polity. And like Griffin, but more explicitly, Manning was worried
about Henry Alline's continuing impact on Nova Scotia and New
Brunswick religious life. As far as Manning was concerned, Alline was
directly responsible for what he once called in 1820, "the flood of
Arminianism" surging through the region. For Manning, Alline's
"errors did not die with him. No, they live to the sorrow of many, and
me among the rest."[53] After re-reading in 1820 Jonathan Scott's bitter
1784 attack of Alline's views, contained in his A Brief View, Manning,
who had once been an ardent New Light and New Dispensationalist,
declared, "I think I could seal Mr S.'s sentiments with my blood."[54] Like
his friend Edmund Reis, Manning passionately believed that the
"preaching which" is "the most blessed is that of the Sovereignty of God

and *total* depravity of man, *that* and *that alone* takes the Crown from the Creature and places it on the Creator."[55] Moreover, it was agreed, in sharp contrast to New Light emotionalism and Allinite mysticism, that a true preacher of the word

should be careful *not to encourage* bodily agitation which profitted little, but strive to inform the understanding more than move the passions, which latter may be done without the mind being informed but much prudence is necessary in so doing, true religion must be *felt* as well as understood. Zeal is very useful and Preachers without it seldom prove beneficial but it should be accompanied with wisdom lest it should do, as it has often done, much harm.[56]

Evangelical religion for Manning was a careful mixture of "informed understanding" and "felt Zeal." And because of the strength of the "New Light – Free Will Baptists" counteroffensive, with its emphasis on the emotions, Manning tended, during the latter part of his life, to stress the central importance of reasoned order.

And if any one person in the first half of the nineteenth century pushed the Nova Scotia Baptist mainstream in the direction of Calvinist order and away from New Light "Free Grace," it was Edward Manning.[57] Until his death in 1851, Manning was widely regarded in the province, and with good reason, as the Baptist Pope. His spiritual hegemony, however, never extended to New Brunswick, or at least much beyond Saint John and Sackville, and this too helps to explain some of the basic differences between the Baptist religious cultures in that province and in Nova Scotia, not only in the nineteenth century, but also in the twentieth. Manning's ordered Baptist Calvinism, it should be stressed, was not only the result of his powerful reaction to the New Dispensationalism and the Allinine-mysticism which he both practised and preached in the 1790s. Nor was it simply Manning's attempt to become both respectable and influential – or as James Innis expressed it in 1805 – that he was a special "Sumbody." Of course, the significance of Manning's determined search for respectability and power should never be underestimated. Nor should his considerable powers of manipulation and influence. But not only did Manning greatly influence others – some would say he stamped his own denomination with his own personal Calvinist, conservative imprint – he also was manipulated and influenced by others. Four Haligonians, in particular, used their prestige and their power to ensure that Manning's Baptist Church was the kind of church they could support. All of these men – J.W. Johnston, who would become premier of Nova Scotia, E.A. Crawley, who became a Baptist minister and educational leader, J.W. Nutting, the prothonotary of the Nova Scotia Supreme Court and John Ferguson, a leading Halifax[58] merchant – had been members of St Paul's Anglican Church, Halifax. A split in this church, between evangelical and non-evangelical factions, resulted in these four men and others leaving the Anglican Church and becoming Baptists. And they brought with them to their new denomination a deepseated Calvinism and an obsession with order and respectability. Their views were widely disseminated in the denomination's weekly, the *Christian Messenger*, edited by Nutting and Ferguson.[59]

Professor Barry Moody has persuasively shown how this small group of new Halifax Baptists pushed the Regular Baptists into support for higher education at Horton Academy and at Acadia University. "It was realized" Moody argues, "that if the Baptists were to attract and hold people of such standing, a more educated clergy would be essential."[60] Such an educated clergy, moreover, would give the denomination badly needed respectability and complete the transfomation of the eighteenth-century sect into the nineteenth-century church. But what Moody refers to as "the 'new' Baptists" did more than this. They also, during the 1840s, played key roles in pushing many Baptists in Nova Scotia from the Reform camp, where they had once huddled, into the Conservative party led by J.W. Johnston.[61] The issue was provincial support for Acadia College; Joseph Howe's opposition to this support, influenced to a great extent by his controversy with the co-editors of the *Christian Messenger*, certainly exacerbated Manning's distrust of the "Tribune of Nova Scotia." In fact, Manning declared in the fall of 1843 that the Almighty "had given Acadia to the Baptists, and they were bound to sustain it. It was an Institution that breathed benevolence, and looked benignly even on those like Howe who have 'a daggar under their coats ready to thrust into it'. . . . It was God's Institution . . . do not let us desert it."[62] The inference was clear in Manning's speech, as Professor J.M. Beck has recently argued;[63] Johnston's Tories "were doing God's work." A half-century earlier, Manning, his associate Harris Harding, Joseph Dimock and his brother James, were just as convinced that the "Devil's work" was being done by the educated ministers of Nova Scotia who were puffed up into minions of anti-Christ by the hubris of their book learning. In the 1840s, Alline's New Light followers, many of whom were to be found in New Brunswick, used these same old shibboleths from the 1790s to condemn "book learning" and all it represented. This New Light "anti-intellectualism" would be a powerful, though gradually diminishing, force in the religious culture of both New Brunswick and Nova Scotia, not only in the nineteenth century but also throughout the twentieth.

The Halifax Baptists obviously found Manning and other members of the Nova Scotia Baptist leadership elite to be surprisingly pliable. And consequently the conservative pro-British bias they enthusiastically endorsed was free to do its "John Bull" work in the Nova Scotia Baptist denomination. This anglicization process was at work at all levels of provincial society. So that by mid-century, because of its influence and because of certain demographic and cultural trends in Nova Scotia, not only did a certain conservative political culture congeal, but also a religious ethos set and set hard, an ethos in which the Regular Baptists were very much at home.

Manning's growing conservatism, a conservatism which gradually became the Baptist mainstream in Nova Scotia, was significantly affected by his negative response to the divisive forces unleashed by the New Dispensation movement in the 1790s, his search for respectability, order, and power, as well as by the growing influence of the Massachusetts-Maine Calvinist Baptists, and after 1825, of the so-called "New Halifax Baptists." But there was an event which occurred in New Brunswick in the first decade of the nineteenth century which played a crucial role in pushing Manning away from what could be called Allinism towards Baptist respectability. In a very real sense this New Brunswick event – a bloody killing – took upon itself tremendous symbolic importance. It represented the logical working out for Manning and others, of New Light extremism and forced them to retreat to the closed Calvinist Baptist approach of the Massachusetts Regular Baptists led by the Reverend Samuel Stillman of Boston, who was determined to make all true Baptists "appear respectable" and also "Calvinist."[64]

Nova Scotia Baptists, in the early nineteenth century, had to work extraordinarily hard to become "respectable." And widely reported events occurring in neighbouring New Brunswick did not make things any easier – something Manning would never forget. In the spring of 1804, a revival occurred in the Shediac area of New Brunswick among the few Baptists living in that region. A few months later, a young woman, Sarah Babcock, encouraged by the itinerant Baptist preacher Jacob Peck, began to prophesy and proclaimed that the end of the world was imminent. And just before the Lord returned, she and Peck were to convert all the Acadians in the neighbourhood. Sarah's father, Amasa, was very much affected by his daughter and the evidence suggests that her message plunged him into insanity. On February 13, 1805, while grinding wheat in his handmill, Amasa took his flour and sprinkled it all over the kitchen floor, declaring boldly "This is the bread of Heaven." He then took off his shoes and rushed out of the door into the deep snow, yelling as he ran, "The world is coming to an end, and the stars are falling." On returning to his house, he lined up his entire family, his wife and nine children, and his sister Mercy and brother Jonathan, and demanded that they sit on a bench while he sharpened a long "clasp knife." After the knife was sharpened, Amasa walked towards his sister, Mercy, and ordered her to take off all her clothes and fall on her knees and ready herself for immediate death and eternity. He next ordered his brother Jonathan to strip and like his sister, Jonathan eagerly obeyed his older brother.

Amasa looked out of the window a number of times, clutched his knife and yelled out "The Cross of Christ" and stabbed his sister fatally. As soon as Jonathan "saw the blood flow," he regained his "senses" and rushed out of the door, naked. Eventually, some neighbours came to the Babcock house and on seeing them, Amasa cried out "Gideon's men arise." But there was no opposition and after having his arms securely tied, Amasa was taken away, obviously insane. He was eventually tried for murder, in Dorchester, and hanged on June 28.[65] The Saint John *Gazette* of June 24 had reported about that trial that

It appeared in evidence that for some time before the trial, the prisoner with several of his neighbours had been in the habit of meeting under a pretense of religious exercises at each other's houses, at which one Jacob Peck, a well known Baptist was a principal performer; That they were under strong delusions and conducted themselves in a very frantic, irregular and even impious manner, and that in consequence of some pretended prophecies by some of the company in some of their pretended religious phrenzies against the unfortunate deceased: the prisoner was probably induced to commit the horrid, barbarous and cruel murder of which he was convicted. The concourse of the people at the trial was very great, who all appeared to be satisfied of the justice of the verdict and sentence.[66]

The "Babcock Tragedy," as it was called, was not, as has been suggested, merely a New Brunswick manifestation of the New Dispensation movement. Similar unfortunate and embarrassing incidents sometimes occurred in other areas of North America as the Christian gospel was twisted beyond recognition and as the dynamics of sectarianism shattered sanity. The "Babcock Tragedy" was such an event, uninfluenced by what had gone on in the Annapolis Valley a decade earlier and an excellent example of how morbid introspection could sometimes be channelled into bloody violence.

Yet, the "Babcock Tragedy" did significantly affect Manning; there is no question of this. Long after the event, Manning referred to it as a dangerous example of "Religious Phrenzy" and gave it equal weight with the New Dispensation movement in accounting for his own espousal of Calvinism and the closed communion Regular Baptists.[67]

It would be a mistake, however, to stress Manning's overall importance at the expense of all other personalities and issues and developments in explaining the differences which have and which now exist between the New Brunswick and Nova Scotia Baptists. Manning's influence, without question, was significant. But other considerations must also be taken into account both within and outside the religious context. For example, New England Calvinist Baptists had, for a variety of reasons, closer ties to Nova Scotia than to New Brunswick. The Reverend Stillman's influence on Thomas Chipman was great at the turn of the eighteenth century and Chipman in turn was instrumental in pushing many New Lights in the Baptist direction. And moreover, the visits of the Maine Baptist evangelists, the Reverends Isaac Case, Daniel Merrill, and Henry Hale, in the post-1800 period, consolidated the Calvinist Baptist position in Nova Scotia and helped immeasurably in transforming New Lights into Regular Baptists.[68] It is noteworthy that these three Baptist ministers had far less of an impact on New Brunswick, especially during the first decade of the nineteenth century – the decade of the "Great Reformation" and the Second Great Awakening.

In New Brunswick, on the other hand, as Stephen Marini has sensitively suggested, radical evangelicalism gained ground during the early decades of the nineteenth century as the frontier of radical sectarianism was pushed northeastward into Maine and to neighbouring New Brunswick.[69] The Christian Church, for example, which according to a key leader, Elias Smith, resolved "to leave behind everything in name, doctrine or practice, not found in the new testament,"[70] made note worthy gains in New Brunswick. And eventually, the Christians merged, in a sense, with the Free Will Baptists. The Christians never exerted the same kind of impact on Nova Scotia religious development and their radical, almost republican sectarianism, would be anathema to a person like Edward Manning. But it would appeal to many New Lights, especially those in New Brunswick who were not part of the rush towards Baptist, Calvinist respectability.

In a very real sense, then, American, especially New England radical sectarian influences appear to have been far more important in New Brunswick[71] than in Nova Scotia where British Baptist and Massachusetts Calvinist Baptist influences were of greater consequence. The Nova Scotia Regular Baptists, moreover, from 1800 on were led by and large, by a small group of extremely able leaders, men like Harris Harding, Thomas Handley Chipman, James and Edward Manning, who were able to make the Nova Scotia Baptist Church what they wanted it to be. And thus the denomination almost became an organizational extension of their collective personalities. New Brunswick Baptists, on the other hand, at the formative stage of existence of their church, lacked such a group of "patriarchs." Without such firm and respected leadership, the New Brunswick Baptists remained largely divided and largely sectarian. And only slowly, as the century unfolded, would the denomination take effective form and the Nova Scotia influence became increasingly important.

VI

There is a second way in which the Allinite New Light legacy also affected the region. As might have been expected, the so-called "ravishing New Birth experience" provided the central core of Alline's preaching and his theology. By pumping mystical and what he called "Free grace" enthusiasm into the neo-Whitefieldian evangelical paradigm, Alline shaped the peculiar brand of Maritime "spiritual individualism" which would significantly affect the religious culture of the region. His was a religion, or more accurately a way of life, which was preoccupied with the individual's special and ongoing personal relationship with Christ and concern with eternal verities – rather than with here-and-now and ephemeral societal problems. Clearly seeing himself as being very much involved in a bitter cosmic struggle between the forces of evil – as represented by Satan, and the forces of righteousness – as personified in Christ, Alline and his thousands of followers had little real interest in achieving "impossible dreams" on earth. Their "New Jerusalem," in other words, was to be located in the Almighty's heaven and not in Nova Scotia or in New Brunswick. Alline had absolutely no desire, nor was he tempted, to develop a mature and sophisticated social and political ethic which could either influence or challenge institutions and power relationships.

In neighbouring New England, as Professor J.L. Thomas has suggestively argued, the post 1820 period witnessed the transformation of the old neo-Whitefieldian individualistic evangelical impulse into a creative social reform thrust. The new social concern emphasized the regeneration of the entire social order by "immediate action" aimed at freeing individuals from what Thomas calls "the restraints of institutions and precedent." Maritime evangelicals in the nineteenth century, especially those directly and indirectly influenced by Alline, neither experienced this secularization of their faith nor the metamorphosis of their entire value-structure. They obviously were largely unaffected by the so-called "theological revolution" which Thomas and others have maintained was at the cutting edge of northern reform. Nor did "romantic perfectionalism" or "post-Millennial optimism" energize Alline's gospel or the nineteenth-century Maritime evangelical social conscience.[72] Alline's conviction that personal salvation should be man's only concern became the evangelical norm; there was little interest therefore in attempting to perfect man and Maritime society. As Alline had once explained it in his *Two Mites:*

You are to consider yourself with a few Hours of Probation cut out of eternal NOW; neither elected nor reprobate, but with electing Love all around you . . . consider neither Time past nor time to come but one Eternal NOW, consider that with God there is neither Succession nor Progression; but that with Him the Moment He said let us make Man, and the Sound of the last Trumpet, is the very same instant, and your Death as much first as your Birth . . . with God all things are Now . . . as the center of a Ring, which is as near to one side as the other.[73]

There was, according to the Alline grasp of spiritual reality, a special sense of urgency for men and women to be redeemed by "the Electing Love of God" since the instant moment of conversion was really an endless eternity. Within Alline's cosmic drama, the shrill shibboleths of social and political reform were meaningless and empty noises. An Allinite other-worldliness, linked to "spiritual individualism," certainly discouraged the coming into existence of any strong evangelical social ethic and social concern. Regenerating individuals, it was contended, could only produce a more humane society; regenerating society, through structural and political reform, was therefore regarded as being both anti-Christian and humanly and institutionally impossible.

4

Revivalism and the Maritime Baptist Tradition

The evangelical style, it is clear, had a singular influence in shaping the contours of Nova Scotian religion during the century following the outbreak of the American Revolution. There were frequent religious revivals during this period, revivals which affected most Protestant Churches and most regions of the province. Not only were there revivals, there were at least three "major reformations" – as contemporaries referred to them – revitalization movements – to use Anthony Wallace's suggestive terminology. These so-called "spiritual earthquakes"[1] – The First and Second Great Awakenings in particular – were the religious means whereby thousands of Nova Scotia New Lights were transformed into Baptists – and Henry Alline's eighteenth-century sect transformed into the frequently warring Free Will and Calvinist Baptist factions.

I

What is particularly noteworthy and somewhat puzzling in contemporary Canadian society is that this revival tradition has apparently had so little formative impact on the way in which many leading and articulate Nova Scotians perceive themselves or view their religion. And certainly the revival-revitalization tradition which was of such great consequence in nineteenth-century Nova Scotia has gone largely unnoticed in central Canada and the west. For most central Canadians and westerners, the Maritime provinces continue to be social, economic, intellectual and even religious backwaters of despair. Events of national consequence, or so the argument goes, have passed the Atlantic region by. Most Canadians are a people obsessed with size and abundance and with a dynamic western thrust into the interior of North America. The Maritime provinces in general and Nova Scotia in particular cannot be fitted into this framework of success and growth.[2]

In recent years I have become increasingly interested in the relationship of so-called evangelical Christianity in the United States and the evolution of American political culture as well as in the possible symbiotic relationship between evangelical Christianity in Nova Scotia and the province's cultural and political values. Most American scholars see an important link between evangelical Christianity and American society and many, moreover, are not afraid to probe into the core of this fascinating relationship. It is clear, as William G. McLoughlin has perceptively argued in *Revivals, Awakenings, and Reform*, that the evangelical tradition has been and continues to be a formative force in American life.[3] For example, one cannot understand the essential nature of the American Revolution without first coming to grips with the spiritual and ideological underpinning of the First Great Awakening. Nor can one appreciate the complex strands of pre-Civil War reform, without realizing how significant the Second Great Awakening was. And, furthermore, it may be argued that Ronald Reagan and much of American neo-conservatism owe a great deal of their influence, if not their substance, to what has been often referred to as the "Fourth Great Awakening."

Yet in Canada there has been, to my knowledge, little serious attempt made to explore the often fascinating connection between evangelical religion and evolving Canadian society. Certainly, I know of no recent or even older study that has looked at Nova Scotia or New Brunswick in this light. It is as though there is no interest in examining a possible relationship or else a sophisticated realization that there is none. But even if there is none (and the available evidence would suggest that there, in fact, is) then some scholar or scholars should be trying to explain why there is none. Canadians are always preoccupied with things American. Since the beginning of the century it has been claimed that American popular culture "deepened the Canadian tendency to think of Canadian problems in American terms, and intensified the Canadian conviction that the continent was an integrated whole." Consequently Canadians "were rendered incapable of resisting the notion that the continent" was a "seamless whole." And in "this manner," it has been suggested by Professor Allan Smith, "the way was prepared for the triumph of the continentalist ideology in the twentieth century."[4]

But despite the reality of Americanization, the so-called "evangelical factor" in Canada has never received the same serious scholarly attention that it has received in American literature. It may be that some Canadian scholars are not eager to be associated with a group which has unacceptable intellectual roots or perhaps is too closely tied to too many unpopular causes. Moreover, it may be argued, few evangelical scholars or scholars sympathetic to the evangelical viewpoint in Canada have developed a deep concern about the way in which the Canadian historical past has shaped the present. Or if they have, they have largely kept their insights to themselves.

The strength and weakness of the evangelical tradition in Canada, in general, and the Baptist tradition in Nova Scotia, in particular, are, in my view, deserving of serious scholarly attention. They must be seen of course, within the framework of contemporary Canadian and North American values. But they must also be explained within a historical context – one which includes the century of revivals, revivalists, and spiritual awakenings which connect Henry Alline to the 1850s, when, it has been argued the political and social culture of the province set and set hard.

II

Exhorting, it may be argued, was far more influential than Biblical preaching in actually bringing about and sustaining religious revivals in Nova Scotia during the immediate post-Alline period. Exhortation – a complex mix of personal testimony, introspective prayer, both articulated and unspoken concern for the spiritual welfare of one's friends and neighbours, tears, sobs, and often other forms of frenzied emotional behaviour – became a vitally significant ingredient in the colony's evangelical religious culture. Preaching from a verse of scripture, but not from a prepared text, was the usual means whereby people in the congregation, young and old, male and female, rich and poor, sensitive and insensitive, were compelled to confront, in a general almost impersonal manner, the inevitability of death, the eternal reality of heaven and hell, the need for salvation, and the crucial role played by Christ in linking the redeemed to the omnipotent and omniscient Almighty. Extemporaneous preaching helped to create a mood of anticipation; it also helped to focus the attention of the audience on those spiritual issues which preoccupied the preacher. To personalize these issues and to drive the jagged edges of their stark reality into the "minds and hearts" of the listeners, a special time of "exhortation" was always set aside at the end of each New Light and early Baptist meeting. And, sometimes, especially in the white heat of revival, the exhortation period stretched into the early morning hours. Anyone moved by the Holy Spirit could and did exhort. Exhortation, it should be stressed, was definitely not something carefully reserved for the male leaders of the congregation – whether elders, deacons, or ministers. Rather, it was the readily available means whereby ordinary people, men, women and even children, could witness publically to their faith and, moreover, could attempt to precipitate conversions. They could, in other words, assert their own intrinsic value, test their spiritual gifts, embellish their preacher's gospel, and attempt to change their communities' values. And, perhaps of greater importance, exhortation gave them an opportunity to participate fully, creatively, and as equals, in what most contemporaries agreed was a movement not only of provincial consequence but also of North American consequence.

Henry Alline, it is clear, established what may be described as the "exhortation paradigm" which his followers and many other evangelicals imposed, in the post Revolutionary period, upon the religious life and practice of Nova Scotia and New Brunswick. Alline, however, was not creating something that was unique to his time and his location; rather he was applying, in his own peculiar manner, a New England New Light practice from the First Great Awakening and shaping it to meet the special exigencies produced by Nova Scotia's First Awakening.

The first detailed description of the important role of exhortation in Alline's ministry is to be found in his *Journal* entry for November 20, 1782. After making brief stops at Yarmouth, Barrington, Ragged Islands, and Sable River, Alline had finally arrived at Liverpool. He observed:

Almost all the town assembled together, and some that were lively christians prayed and exhorted, and God was there with a truth. I preached every day and sometimes twice a day; and the houses where I went were crowded almost all the time. Many were brought out of darkness and rejoiced, and exhorted in public.[5]

Alline was particulary moved by a "young lad" who took "his father by the hand," and cried out, "O father, you have been a great sinner, and now are an old man: an old sinner, with grey hairs upon your head, going right down to destruction." "O turn, turn, dear father," the son implored "return and fly to Jesus Christ." There were according to Alline "many other such like expressions and entreaties, enough to melt a stony heart."[6]

There are, at least, three notable characteristics of exhortation in Alline's description, all of which became integral to New Light and Baptist early worship practice. First, there was a close linking of prayer and exhortation yet a clear distinction between the two was, nevertheless, drawn. Prayer was oriented towards God while exhortation was specifically directed at friends, neighbours, and associates. Second, it was not unusual for children to take the initiative and also to point their spiritual concern at their parents. Such a public act must have been permeated not only by paradox but also by bitter irony, traditional deference being shattered as the young arrogantly led the old to salvation. Third, the verbal exhortation was often accompanied by the touching of hands, as flesh met flesh, and as concern and love was expressed by close human contact. It is of some consequence that one of Alline's most vociferous critics, Jonathan Scott, denounced him for encouraging his followers to "caress" one another by bombarding "The *Passions* of the *young*, ignorant, and inconsiderate" with the pernicious "Sound and Gingle of Words."[7]

It would be a serious mistake, however, to give the impression that Alline both encouraged and facilitated the growth of "frenzied exhortation." Nothing could have been further from the reality of actual practice or of Alline's own view. Alline, as has already been pointed out, was suspicious of what he called "counterfeit" zeal and he constantly chastized his immature followers for being "so fond of everything that appears like the power of God, that they receive almost anything that has zeal." It was therefore essential to distinguish clearly between "false zeal" based upon "nothing but a spirit of self" and "true zeal" based upon "the spirit of God" and which, moreover "brings meekness, love and humility with the zeal."[8] For Alline, exhortation was not to be a wild uncontrolled exhibition of religious enthusiasm. Rather, it was to be a carefully controlled means of personalizing and focusing the Christian message and also an opportunity for those who felt called to preach the gospel to test their gift and to gain valuable experience. It should surprise no one, therefore, that Thomas Handley Chipman and John Payzant, preachers who travelled with Alline, who exhorted after Alline's sermons, and who proudly carried his tradition into the nineteenth-century, were almost pathologically opposed to emotional excesses.

Not all of Alline's followers, however, shared totally this preoccupation with good order but even those who were suspicious of extreme emotionalism placed heavy emphasis on the crucial importance of exhortation. Joseph Dimock, for example, who had been converted in 1787, at the age of nineteen, and who served as minister of the Chester Baptist Church from 1793 until his death in 1846, believed that exhorting was far more effective than preaching. He observed, for example, in 1797:

People were loath to leave our place of public worship. I mostly conversed freely after the meeting with those that are under conviction, and others that give the opportunity, and I have found freedom in thus conversing. When I take persons by the hand and speak to them they know that I mean *them*, while preaching in public may be turned on others, and I have thought that God blessed this particular addressing of individuals more than all the preaching.[9]

For Dimock, exhorting was simply the "particular addressing of individuals" – both by word and by touch – and these sessions went on "for one, two, or three hours," right into the middle of the night. These marathon meetings must have both exhausted and exhilarated those who were present – breaking down inhibitions, helping to exacerbate guilt, exaggerating fears and anxieties, and sharpening the edges of expectations. Often those who remained to be exhorted in house, barn or meeting house, spent hours on their knees; their faces, bathed in tears, reflected in and distorted by the flickering tongues of candles, while they desperately tried to create some flashes of light in the black sea of darkness. The eerie light, the often strange cacophony of sounds, the intense physical intimacy, the suggestibility produced by exhaustion and emotional excitement, the smell of bodies under stress, all of these factors combined to produce a mood of expectation. And preachers like Dimock were able to transform this expectation into intense conversion experiences. For Dimock – as he once eloquently put it – "felt a weight of truths that flowed right from the eternal God into my soul, which has enabled me to communicate to others a sense of God and eternal things." "It seemed as though God was so near" at these exhortation sessions to Dimock's "soul – yea – all around me – that I could see him in everything I beheld."[10] The Almighty was there in the candle light, in the stuttered murmurs of conviction, in the smells produced by bodies, building, and clothes. As had been the case with Alline, all sensory perceptions, all available stimulii, were used to draw people to "the Heavenly Charmer."

A decade later, during the "Great Reformation," in Liverpool, Nova Scotia, exhorting was widely perceived as being a key factor in bringing about the widespread revival. According to Nancy De Wolf, a resident of Liverpool in 1807, the revival was "the most powerful reformation I ever was witness to." The forty-three year old woman, who had been converted at Annapolis Royal by Harris Harding and Joseph Dimock in 1789, went on to describe what she referred to as the new "Penticost."

for about a fortnight it was a sabath all over Liverpool, all Labour ceased, vessels stopt loading, stores were shut up and all were enquiring what they should do to be saved, the meeting houses [Methodist and Congregational] were often open night and day; indeed every house was a meeting house by turns for the power of God would strike them in their own houses and they would be Converted in a few hours time and go right to their companion or neighbour and say God has redeemed my soul. He has taken me out of the Horrible Pit and mirey clay and put a new song into my mouth, even praise to God, Come my dear friend share a part their is room enough in my fathers kingdom.

Throughout Liverpool "little children" were "lisping out the praises of God."[11]

Another eye witness, the Reverend John Payzant, noted that during the 1807 "Reformation," the "old, and young, experienced the love of God" and "went and ex[h]orted from House, to House and Telling what great [things] the Lord had done for them." Then on March 3, at the conclusion of a "night meeting at the Meeting-House," after the "sermon was ended," many people in the congregation spontaneously started to exhort and to witness "either Crying for mercy under a Since of their parishing condition, or rejoicing and blessing God, for his Goodness to them" They seemed to speak with one voice as they declared that "the Lord has appeared and deliver'd my Soul, he has made an everlasting Covenant with my soul. I shall sign with him to all Eternity." The unconverted were singled out for special individual attention; names would be used, fingers pointed, as friends and neighbours were urged "to come, and pertake with them" of salvation. The unredeemed were told that "there was mercy for them, for they had been the worst of Siners." On confessing "their bad deeds," and after describing the precise nature of their "New Birth," the newly converted immediately turned to those persons "that they had anything against" and "asked their pardon." "All offences were made up," in the catharsis of individual salvation and community revival.[12] Thus, what Victor Turner has called "the ecstacy of spontaneous communitas" was channelled into "something profoundly communal and shared."[13]

What was originally spontaneous with respect to exhortation soon became ritualized church polity. By the end of the first decade of the nineteenth century in Nova Scotia, in most of the New Light Baptist churches, exhortation was probably as important a feature of worship as was preaching or praying or singing. Usually exhortation took place after the extemporaneous sermon; often exhortation blended into prayer or prayer became exhortation and also, frequently, the singing of spiritual songs or hymns added both emotional substance and theological richness and diversity to the experience. In some churches lay people – usually six or eight of them – took the lead in exhorting others in the congregation. In other churches, exhorting was clearly the responsibility of the ordained minister and sometimes an elder. It is interesting to note that when the Maine Baptist itinerants Isaac Case and Henry Hale visited Nova Scotia in 1807 and later, they took turns in exhorting and in preaching. When Hale, for example, preached to a Baptist congregation, Case usually exhorted at the end of the service. And their roles were often reversed at the next meeting.[14]

By 1810, "amateur exhorters" were being replaced in some regions of Nova Scotia and New Brunswick by "professional" ones. There are four possible explanations for this development. First, the "amateur exhorters" were losing their earlier intense enthusiasm and were beginning to repeat themselves. And this repetitiveness was often both embarrassing and spiritually unenlightening for those who had to endure listening to the almost meaningless shibboleths. Second, there was, among Nova Scotia Baptists, a growing preoccupation with order and respectability. And there was, moreover, a widespread concern, especially among the ministerial elite, that lay exhortation too often led to emotional excesses – excesses which brought opprobrium to the evangelical cause in Nova Scotia. Ministerial leaders (Thomas Handley Chipman and Edward Manning, in particular) were keen to transform their New Light sect into a respectable Baptist denomination. Chipman, whose attitude to good order had been shaped both by Alline and the Reverend Samuel Stillman, the minister of the First Baptist Church, Boston, had emphasized, as early as 1799, that he keenly wished to "appear as respectable."[15] He did not want to be a "nobody"[16] in a peripheral sect but rather a "somebody" in a major denomination. And Edward Manning, of course, enthusiastically endorsed this position. One of his New Light critics, James Innis, had pointed out in 1805 that Manning "thought himself Sumbudy but I was nothing and less than nothing."[17]

Third, there is much evidence to suggest that by 1810, the ministerial elite, the Mannings, Theodore Seth Harding, and T.H. Chipman, in particular, wished to establish their authority over their denomination and also to assert their ministerial power. They were eager, in other words, to control effectively all aspects of their congregational life – particularly worship and especially exhortation. By weakening lay involvement and itineracy, and by dominating church life, the ministers underscored their professionalism and their desire to transfer the allegiance of Alline's sect to their own unique church.[18] For Manning and others, New Light enthusiasts like James Innis obviously represented a sectarian past which they wished to forget; by stressing their attachment to Alline, itinerants like Innis touched a raw nerve in people like Edward Manning and Theodore Seth Harding whose abandonment of Allinite principles had created a certain emotional emptiness in their religious lives.

The fourth reason for what might almost be called the professionalization of exhortation, was the conservative New England Baptist influence. Three Maine Baptist missionaries, in particular, Isaac Case, Henry Hale, and Daniel Merrill, significantly influenced Baptist life and practice in Nova Scotia in the 1807–10 period – and beyond. Among other things, they pushed the somewhat reluctant Nova Scotia Baptists into a Calvinist and "closed communion" direction. Reacting against not only the significant inroads being made by Free Will Baptists in their region but also attacks from the Congregational establishment, these Baptist leaders were preoccupied with finding a middle ground between Alline-Free Will religious enthusiasm on the one hand and structured worship on the other. Viewing New England and Nova Scotia-New Brunswick as a seamless whole, they fitted their matrix of values and beliefs on people on both sides of the border. Their Yankee order soon began to neutralize New Light spontaneity. And this trend, together with the continuing anglicization of the colony, as represented by the influx of thousands of immigrants from Great Britain, did much to ensure that the mainstream of Nova Scotia Baptists drifted away from its Allinite traditions.[19]

By the time of the outbreak of the War of 1812, it may be argued, the so-called Alline-New Light exhortation element of Nova Scotia's evangelical religious culture had been significantly altered by evolving events and personalities. Nevertheless, exhortation, however distorted, remained an important ingredient in Baptist worship and practice throughout the early decades of the nineteenth century.

Exhortation may be perceived as a special "ritual" whereby, as Victor Turner[20] has brilliantly argued, "well-bonded" human beings have created "by structural means – spaces and times in the calendar or, in the cultural cycles of their most cherished groups which cannot be captured" in what he calls the "classificatory nets of their routinized spheres of action." "By verbal and non-verbal means," exhortation was the means whereby many Nova Scotians were able to break away from their "innumerable constraints and boundaries" and capture what has been called the "floating world" of creativity and self-discovery. People, according to Turner, alternate between "fixed" and "floating" worlds; they oscillate, in other words, between, on the one hand, preoccupation with order and constraints and, on the other, a search for novelty and freedom. New Light exhortation was the occasion for thousands of Nova Scotians to experience what has been called an "anti-structural liminality." It became a symbol of the social and religious mood in which all sorts of hitherto internalized and sublimated desires, dreams, hopes, and aspirations became legitimized. Women, for example, broke through the hard shell of deference to express deeply felt feelings and to criticize their husbands; children often demanded obedience from their parents. Traditional behaviour and values were challenged; the "anti-structural liminality" of the exhortation ritual helped to give shape and form, however transitory, to a profoundly satisfying "tender, silent, cognizant mutuality." In a sense, this aberrant behaviour may be regarded as "rituals of status reversal." "Cognitively," as Turner points out, "nothing underlines regularity as well as absurdity or paradox" and "emotionally nothing satisfies as much as extravagant or temporarily permitted illicit behaviour." The rituals of status reversal, moreover, as seen in exhortation, not only challenged community values but also sub-consciously reaffirmed the hierarchical principle still undergirding society.

There was, it should also be stressed, an intensely satisfying and intensely pleasurable feeling of Christian fellowship as the "ecstacy of spontaneous communitas" virtually overwhelmed the congregation. The "spontaneous communitas" produced by the exhortation experience had something almost " 'magical' about it." People, despite themselves, shared a "feeling of endless power"; and this feeling was both exhilarating and frightening. They were drawn by the "mystery of intimacy" towards one another – as Christian love challenged what seemed to be a selfish, limited, almost worldly, fidelity. They saw Christ in their friends and their neighbours and they wanted desperately to love their friends as they loved Christ. Some did – for a moment – and the joy must have been glorious. They also realized that "spontaneous communitas" was only "a phase, a moment, not a permanent condition" as "the mystery of distancing and of 'tradition' " regained firm control of their hearts and minds.[21] But it was a return to the status quo with a difference. For things had changed despite the power of the forces of continuity; religious life in Nova Scotia was an ongoing process – a process which would be affected by other rituals, by other people and by other symbols at other times.

III

Nova Scotia's Second Great Awakening, it may be argued, stretched from the late 1790s to approximately 1810. And the 1806–8 period marked the spiritual and emotional peak of the revitalization movement. The Awakening in Nova Scotia and also in New Brunswick coincided with a similar religious movement sweeping through northern New England and other regions of the United States, as well as "Upper Canada." The Nova Scotia Second Awakening, it is clear, was an integral part of a North American Awakening; there was a regular and steady flow of preachers moving both ways across the border and to them the area was a seamless whole and the Awakening a spiritual movement which could not be restrained by national boundaries.

It seems obvious that a variety of socio-economic interpretations could also be applied to the Second Great Awakening in Nova Scotia. It could be seen as a social movement "continued" by Allinite revivalists who were trying to emulate their master. Or it could be viewed as an emotional reaction to the forces of economic and demographic change then engulfing Nova Scotia. The coming of some 20,000 Loyalists and thousands of Scots had fundamentally altered the human face of the colony. Or the Awakening could be regarded as the traditional out-settlement protest directed at Halifax or else the socio-psychological means whereby the sect mentality was transformed into the Church.

Yet what particularly distinguishes the Second from the First Awakening is the striking absence of one charismatic preacher who almost single-handedly coaxes the movement into existence, and then affects its development. Of course, the principal actors in the unfolding drama of the "Second Great Awakening" as well as crucial human links connecting Henry Alline's New Light movement with the evolving Baptist Church were preachers like Harris Harding, Joseph Dimock, Edward and James Manning, and Thomas Handley Chipman – all early and all enthusiastic disciples of the Falmouth preacher at least until the turn of the century.[22]

What is noteworthy in the "Second Awakening" is the key role played by children and women in bringing about various local revivals and also in affecting their emotional and ideological substance. Over and over again the local church records, whether in Cornwallis, Liverpool, or Yarmouth, as well as the reports written by the revivalists themselves, underscore the importance of children and women. For example, in December 1806, Chipman reported to the readers of the *Massachusetts Baptist Missionary Magazine* that he had been in the Yarmouth-Argyle region for five weeks and that "such glorious times I never saw before." "Multitudes are turned to God," he observed. "I cannot with ink and pen . . . describe the one half God has done." Chipman went on:

Since the work began (three months ago), there have been about one hundred and fifty souls brought to own Jesus, as their rightful Lord and sovereign king. . . . We have had two church meetings, and surely I never saw such meetings before. It was indeed the house of God, and the very gate of heaven. The last Saturday we began at ten in the morning, and continued until eight in the evening, to hear persons relate the dealings of God with their souls, and then a great number were prevented for want of time. . . .

A great many of the subjects of this work have been young people and children. Seldom a meeting but some are brought to embrace the offers of life; sometimes five, six, and seven at a meeting. There are meetings in some parts of the town almost every day.[23]

In March 1807, the Reverend John Payzant, Alline's brother-in-law, and the only ordained New Light Minister in Nova Scotia who had stubbornly refused to become a Baptist, noted that a number of women and young people on the geographical periphery of Liverpool had experienced conversion and were moving from "House to House and telling what great [things] the Lord had done for them." There were nightly meetings and the "young people" were especially active. But Payzant was not at all involved at this early stage in what he described as "a wonderful moving [among the people] of the power of God." Finally, on March 3, what Payzant referred to as "the fire" began "to kindle" and "the flame" to engulf his Meeting House.

At night meeting . . . as soon as the Sermon was ended the people began to Shout from all sides of the House, either Crying for mercy under a Since of their parishing condition; or rejoicing and blessing God, for his Goodness to them. The Sinners were cut down by the all mighty power of God, under a Since that the[y] were in a ruined condition, and the Lord has appeared for a number of them, their language was the Lord has appeared and delivered my soul, he has made an everlasting convenant with my Soul. I shall reign with him to all eternity . . . and as soon as any one came out, they would call to others to come and partake with them, telling them that there was mercy for them, for they had been the worst of Sinners. And acknowledging all their bad deeds, and if there were any person that they went to, and asked their pardon, all offences were made up, and the meeting continued till day. The number that experienced the love of God on their hearts are not yet ascertained. There were more than 20 that came out clear; but it is thought by Some that Stade all night, that there was more than 50 who experienced the love of God.

The next day, by the break of day, the Streets were full of people, of all descriptions, and it appears that there was ten times as many people in the place as before. So it continued all day they going from house to house. There was no business done that week and but little victuals dressed. The people were So many for there was old and young, rich and poor, male and female, Black and White, all met together and appeared to be as one. At night they came into the meeting House in that manner; the meeting House echo'd with their Praises and rejoicing. So that there was no publick Singing or Prayers but the whole night was Spent in that manner. It was judged that there was above 1,000 people.[24]

After the meeting, the assembled throng went from house to house. They were led by "Many Small Boys and Girls, Some of them telling the goodness of God, others in distress." Exhausted, conscience-stricken, introspective, yet enjoying their unexpected influence and power, the young inhabitants of Liverpool continued to witness during the day and to meet together at night. The adults at the evening meeting complained of the constant noise and the yelling. They wanted to hear sermons and, moreover, they demanded order. The young, enjoying immensely their new-found power and authority, refused to abandon what they considered to be practices sanctioned by the Holy Spirit.

At the end of March, forty-four joined the church. At that special service, "more than 1,000 people" attended. The entire next week "was spent in having meetings, every night, the young people meet[ing] in various places, for they were too numerous to meet in one place." "Whenever a number of them met together," it was noted, "the time was spent Singing Hymns and praying."[25]

The meetings continued until August when Harris Harding arrived. Harding obviously wanted to make Baptists of all the new converts. Payzant vociferously opposed the move and the "Reformation" was replaced by bitter sectarian strife. Some – according to Payzant – were "dipped in bitter water for Baptism;" "It appeared" he maintained, "that they thought that to dip people in water was all the religion that was needful."[26]

There is yet another way to look at the Second Awakening – this time from the perspective of a backslider and from a woman. Nancy Lawrence (1764–1807) was born in Lincoln, Massachusetts, and her career provides fascinating evidence of individual conversion, declension, and revival.[27] Nancy's father, the Reverend William Lawrence (1723–80) a distinguished Harvard graduate, was an eminent Congregational minister who had opposed, throughout his lifetime, religious enthusiasm of any kind.

Sometime in 1788 or in early 1789, Nancy came to Granville, near Annapolis, to visit her Loyalist brother William and sister-in-law who had recently moved to the township. While in Granville Nancy became an ardent New Light, having been influenced by Harris Harding and Joseph Dimock in particular. She felt compelled to share immediately her new found faith with her friends and her family; and it was a faith not insignificantly shaped by Henry Alline's theology.

Nancy had been overwhelmed by "the riches of free grace" to such an extent that, without her mother's consent, she abandoned her spinster status in December for marriage to a widower with three young children. Her husband James DeWolf, a merchant from Horton, had according to Nancy "a double claim to my affections, for he loves Jesus, we have a spiritual union that earth nor Hell can never dissolve which will outlive time and exist to all Eternity."[28] After briefly describing her "deceit" to her mother and requesting her "forgiveness" in a letter written on January 5, 1791, Nancy DeWolf quickly turned her attention to what mattered most to her – the salvation of her family and friends. Nancy's obviously distraught mother – a traditional Congregationalist – must have been both angered and amazed to have been instructed by her daughter to tell all their Lincoln neighbours that "they must be born again or I shall be eternally separated from them." "Tell them," she informed her mother "'tis not for any merit or worthiness in me that Lord hath chosen me, no tis free Grace, free Grace and it is free for them as me." "Give my love to Bulkly Adams and wife," she went on "tell him he must forsake all for Christ or He is lost for ever, remember me to all my friends tell them that the friendship of the world is emnity with God, that my soul loves and longs for their redemption."[29]

Nancy DeWolf, by her conversion and her marriage, had obviously declared her independence of her mother and her family. Though happily married, at least for the first few years of her marriage, Nancy found herself estranged from her family – a family which was unable to condone either her religious enthusiasm or her secret marriage to an older man. There is a sense of despair and acute concern in her letter written on May 2, 1793 to her mother. "Tis a year and half since I received a line from the family," she complained "and have only heard from you but once" since early 1790. "I want exceedingly to hear from each one of the family" she confessed, "sometimes my heart forebodes a thousand evils, and imagination points distress and horor around that dwelling where first I received the ellemental life." Eighteen months later, on October 9, 1794, Nancy, informed her mother:

Tis now almost three years since I received a line from any of the family, I conclude you have entirely cast me of[f], but God is my refuge, my refuge, my fortress, high tower and exceeding great reward. He will not leave me nor forsake me.

Nancy still had not heard from her family on April 17, 1795. Her mother, however, was constantly bombarded in the few letters written by Nancy with Allinite statements such as "O that you may have an interest in that Lamb which was slain from before the foundation of the world."[30]

Sometime between April 1796 and November 1798, the DeWolf family moved from Horton – the Allinite New Light heartland – to Liverpool, where the Reverend John Payzant was the Congregational minister. During this period, Nancy evidently lost much of her religious enthusiasm. Her mind, she graphically observed "was carried away, captive into Babalon" and her "harp was hung upon the willows." She now never mentioned "Experimental religion" in her letters to her mother. Rather, she complained bitterly about her poor health and the frequent absences from Liverpool of her husband. "There is nothing but a sciety [anxiety] and trouble in this life," she moaned "and tho we are prospered in our outward circumstances beyond our expectations yet it appears to me all is Vanity and Vexation of Spirit."[31]

All was "Vanity and vexation of Spirit" for Nancy DeWolf until Liverpool's "Great Reformation." Until the early months of 1807, she was evidently far more interested in Liverpool's economic prospects than she was in evangelical Christianity. Then she experienced a profound spiritual revitalization; she had discovered the excitement of her earlier New Light faith.

Like many other Nova Scotians in the first decade of the nineteenth century, Nancy Dewolf had experienced first the ecstacy of regeneration and then the slow and almost inevitable slide to religious apathy and indifference. And then came the revival to be followed, for many, but not for Nancy, who died soon afterwards, by declension and then another outburst of spiritual revitalization.

In early February 1807, Nancy, together with hundreds of her Liverpool neighbours, were caught up in what the Reverend John Payzant described as "a wonderful moving [among the people] of the power of God." For almost two months, Nancy DeWolf attended special revival meetings at least "four or five times a week." And by the first week of April, she had, she was certain, rediscovered the magic of her earlier faith during what she called "a day of Penticost." She wrote to her sister:

it is thought their is five Hundred brought to the knowledge of the truth. I could write a volum but I am affraid I shall frighten you, for I was so far from enjoying religion when I was with you. My mind was carried away captive into Babalon and how could I sing one of Zion's songs in a strange land? My harp was hung upon the willows, but O my sister I can bless God their is a Glorious reallity in experimental Religion. I can say this night with the energy of truth that I am a living witness for the cause of Christ, that we must be born again or never enter the kingdom of Heaven, that we must be slain by the law and made or live by grace. O that it might spread from shore to shore that the knolege of the Lord might cover the earth as the waters do the seas.[32]

For a two week period, Nancy observed, no one worked in Liverpool, since everyone was caught up in the revival. The enthusiasm, energy, and confidence of the young converts struck a particularly responsive chord in Nancy as she remembered those days and months – some two decades earlier – when she, too, had been absolutely certain about the "Glorious reallity" of "experimental Religion." When she heard the young Liverpool converts witness to their faith, she heard her own voice echo from what seemed to be a distant past. She knew the words – she knew the phrases – and she understood the complex nature of the concern – for these were all once uniquely hers. What reverberated through her mind, richocheting wildly into the darkest corners of her guilt, were the familiar – the painfully familiar – reminders of a past when she was convinced that she had suddenly and marvellously, by the ravishing power of the Holy Spirit, been "reinstated in the Image of God." In March and April 1807, the present was collapsed into the past, as Nancy DeWolf confronted the bitter depths of her back-sliding. "God has redeemed my soul," she was told, over and over again, by scores of young people, "He has taken me out of the Horrible Pit and mirey clay and put a new song into my mouth, even praise to God." "Come my dear friend," she was urged "share a part their is room in my fathers kingdom."[33]

It is clear that Nancy DeWolf's experience was not unique. Many Nova Scotians, in the post-Revolutionary period, experienced the ecstacy of conversion, and then the prolonged despair associated with back-sliding. Some, during frequent revivals which affected their communities, would emulate Nancy DeWolf. These people were not reconverted but rather were merely revived. For some, their being regularly revived from what they described as a state of "spiritual stupor" became the essence of their religious experience. Outside stimulii, they felt, were needed to keep the evangelical cause alive; their inner resources appeared to be totally inadequate to accomplish this end. Dependence merely bred further dependence. And this too would become a distinguishing feature of both Nova Scotia and Maritime evangelical religious culture.

IV

It may be argued that during the Awakening there was a "breathtaking reversal of roles" – as normally subservient and passive children and women enthusiastically abandoned their traditional deferential social role in Nova Scotia society to become almost the *de facto* leaders of the community and, in a sense, the unchallenged source of moral and spiritual authority.[34] It was relatively easy for these women and children to contend that they possessed the Holy Spirit and that they were specially selected conduits for the transformation of their communities' values. Revivalists like Harris Harding and Joseph Dimock, in particular, encouraged this development since they believed that it was an important legacy from Henry Alline's time. Apparently, quite a few Nova Scotia children, ranging in age from seven to sixteen, saw in the revivals an excellent opportunity to assert their own sense of worth and self-importance in a society which traditionally relegated them to positions of subservience and acute dependence. Harris Harding once described the confident way in which an eight-year old Ann Eaton related her Christian experience in Yarmouth. "She had given good evidence before this that she was a renewed person," Harding observed, and he then went on

She came forward, and was placed on the communion table (she is very small for her age) the sight moved the people much. She told her experience, answered questions to satisfaction, and was received. The host of people, were loth to leave the meeting. What is the God of heaven doing?[35]

It was a good question but Harding never tried to answer it. All he knew with certainty was that only the Holy Spirit could have transformed the eight-year old Ann Eaton into a mature, sensitive Christian.

There is also some evidence to suggest that many young converts often sharply, and some would say, unfairly, contrasted the rhetoric of community Christian morality with the reality and in the process found their parents disconcertingly wanting. By stressing parental and adult hyprocisy and their own pure motivation, the children, with the explicit encouragement of the revivalists, were able often to become the cutting edge of the revival, pushing it in directions that – some would say – *hubris* and pent-up frustration was relentlessly driving them. It was, for them, obviously, an exciting experience.

Some women, like some children, also used the Awakening to assert their own sense of importance in a world which also seemed to relegate them to positions of inferiority and subservience. In the revival meetings they were given the opportunity to express their most deeply felt feelings and attitudes as equals. They also often appropriated the power to control events; the Holy Spirit, as they saw it, did not distinguish between males and females. In their homes the women, as wives, mothers, sisters, grandmothers, were conditioned to accept their role as second-class citizens; in the revival meetings they emphatically were not. As Donald Mathews has convincingly argued in his fine study, *Religion in the Old South*[36] conversion and revivals provided women in particular with what he refers to as "psychological and social space." Giving up temporarily the traditional web of cultural constraints which significantly affected their behaviour and sense of responsibility, many women sought in revivals the justification for independence and collective support for almost aberrant behaviour. "It was denunciation of the old life," according to Mathews, "and the consequent devaluation of that life," which "was especially resented by worldly husbands who did not share conversion and the conviction that the old life was so bad and did not agree with the idea that their wives may have suffered from it."[37] Many evangelical husbands probably felt the same way, and this reaction would only add to the existing tension and sense of excitement.

The general alienation of the men may have been intensified when they realized that many of the women were almost irresistibly attracted to the visiting revivalists. "The repressed sensuality of a religion which emphasized love, care, and intimate companionship in Christ" it has been asserted "could easily mix sacred and profane desire . . . into a volatile compound that provided women unaccustomed to compassionate, impassioned, even passionate men, such as the clergy seemed to be, with an emotional experience they could not quite fathom, but which they knew excited and fulfilled them."[38]

It should be kept in mind that during the 1790 to 1812 period most of the patriarchs were unusually vigorous and attractive young men. Edward Manning, for example, was a giant of a man – over six feet tall – who, as a teenager had killed three bears in one violent confrontation. Manning was a "man of great courage and muscular force." He and a friend

were once travelling in the woods. His companion had a gun and he a hatchet. They came upon a bear's den in which were three bears, I think one old one and two yearlings. He said that he asked his companion why he did not fire, he said, I am afraid of killing the dogs. Mr. Manning said I would shoot something. I think one of the bears put out its nose, and he cleft its skull, another he struck on the back and severed its backbone so that he told me he could see the heaving of the longues [lungs] through the incision. The third was making off, but he pursued it up a rising ground, and struck the hatchet into its skull, when it screamed out almost like a human being and came tumbling down the hill.[39]

Harris Harding, Joseph Dimock, Thomas Handley Chipman, James Manning, and T.S. Harding were not three-bear men, and they were not as physically imposing as was Edward Manning but, in their prime, they were all unusually warm and affectionate individuals who possessed a powerful appeal over both women and men.

Christian fellowship in the Awakening took on a special meaning; as Mathews has stressed, evangelicals

redefined social relationships in terms of social intimacy, mutual respect, and communal discipline. Intimacy was most dramatically expressed by the many ways in which Evangelicals touched each other, offering the right hand of fellowship almost universally. They often prayed through personal crisis with their arms around each other, and some greeted their brothers and sisters in Christ with a kiss. . . . Perhaps even more intimate than ritualistic touching, however, was public confession of sin and sharing with others the deepest, most private thoughts about oneself and his relationships with other people and with God.[40]

These confessions, which often included fascinating, detailed descriptions of events never previously discussed in public, stripped away the veneer of pious respectability and introduced instead brutally frank honesty which convicted but also titilated. Sometimes women were amazingly explicit about sexual matters and about their morbid introspection. But they were also not afraid to express their sense of spiritual liberation and freedom. They were not ashamed to express deeply felt feelings either by the spoken word or by touch; they needed to communicate their profound Christian love in an environment that both facilitated and encouraged such a development.

A great deal of revival scholarship, it should be stressed, in the United States and Canada, has dealt almost exclusively with the preachers and the message, largely at the expense of the congregations. And when congregations are analyzed, they are usually done so from a distinctly male perspective. It is as if women, children, and young people do not even exist. But they do and the evidence is quite convincing that they made up the vast majority of people affected by the Second Great Awakening in particular and all the Nova Scotia revival. This central fact must inform any sensitive and sophisticated study of Canadian religious revivals and Awakenings.

According to Anthony Wallace, a "Great Awakening" occurs, "when a society finds that its day-to-day behaviour has deviated so far from the accepted (traditional) norms that neither individuals nor large groups can honestly (consistently) sustain the common set of religious understandings by which they believe (have been taught) they should act." A period of "individual stress" – or loss of identity – is followed by one of "cultural distortion" during which the "ordinary stress-reduction techniques fail to help those who react to them." Then there arises a charismatic leader or leaders, people who have undergone the traumatic religious experience "that epitomizes the crisis of the culture." Such leaders, in the fourth stage of the revitalization movement, "begin to attract the more flexible (usually the younger) members of the society, who are willing to experiment with new mazeways or lifestyles." There is often a pulling back to a conservative-negative position and then a sudden leap forward to a new, radically different "world view." Finally, the revivalists succeed in influencing the more passive individuals – and as the collective "mazeways are cleared. . . . Familiar patterns change, sex roles alter," and a new culture clicks into fragile place – based upon the past and the future. And the process repeats itself as each generation attempts to revitalize its way of life.[41]

What is striking is that the Wallace descriptive paradigm can be so easily applied to Nova Scotia's two Great Awakenings. This fact does not necessarily, of course, explain the Awakenings. Nor does it take anything away from the spiritual dimension of revivals. What it does, however, is force any student of revivals to ask often difficult questions of the evidence and also to locate these intriguing events within a much larger comparative framework.

V

Charles G. Finney, the outstanding nineteenth-century American evangelist once observed that "a revival is not a miracle, it consists entirely in the right exercise of the powers of nature. . . . The connection between the right use of means for a revival and a revival is as philosophically sure as between the right use of means to raise grain and a crop of wheat."[42] Not everyone, of course, in the nineteenth century or today would agree with Finney's analysis. But it is clear that as the nineteenth century unfolded in Nova Scotia, an increasing number of Baptist ministers began to feel that they could, as one of them put it, almost "will" a revival into existence.[43] Some obviously needed a revival in order to assert their own spirituality and also their own sense of ministerial importance in a denomination that was rapidly expanding. The older Baptist ministers found themselves in the late 1820s and 1830s and early 1840s challenged by a new group of young evangelists, some of whom were eager to shoulder the backward-looking patriarchs aside in a province that was experiencing what D.C. Harvey once correctly described as an "Intellectual Awakening."[44]

During the so-called "Third Awakening," the Baptist leaders, whether of the new or old generation, stressed the importance of order and respectability. There was "very little disorder to be seen at our meetings," the young Reverend Tupper observed from Aylesford in 1828.[45] The Reverend Joseph Dimock, then sixty-six years of age, reported from Chester six years later, that "There has been great solemnity; great freedom on the part of the converts in telling what the Lord has done for them. There has been no confusion; they have spoken one at a time; no preacher or private Christian has been interrupted in prayer or in speaking."[46] A year later, the recently ordained I.E. Bill wrote from Liverpool that "There was no outcry – no confusion. . . . There has been on those occasions formerly more or less confusion, but now all was perfect stillness."[47] The Calvinist Baptists were obviously trying to distance themselves from the Free Will Baptists who were beginning to make inroads in Nova Scotia and perhaps the Calvinists were also endeavouring to declare their independence of Henry Alline. On August 24, 1821, the Reverend Edward Manning described one chaotic church service:

No sooner was I seated than a young Woman whom I know not, screamed out (from the gallery) and a number below, all females, a melancholy sound to me, because I thought there was such an extravagancy of Voice, and such uncommon gesticulations, leaving their seats, running round the broad Isle, Swinging their Arms, bowing their heads to the Ground, Stretching their hands out right and left, then stretching them up as high as they could while the head was bowed down to the floor almost. . . . The young woman up in the gallery came directly to me with an awfully dis-Figured face, screeching verry loud, indeed calling me brother, O my brother O my brother! until she was exhausted and then she turned away.[48]

According to Manning, "Allinism" had made people in the Horton area "generally . . . more confounded than comforted."[49] Manning felt it was essential for his Baptists to define their separate collective identity by behaving in a radically different manner than the Allinite Free Will Baptists. He did not want to abandon the neo-Whitfieldian tradition; what he wished to do was to get rid of, once and for all, what he considered to be New Light excesses.

It may be of some interest that in my examination of hundreds of local Baptist revivals in Nova Scotia in the post-1830 period, I have yet to find one characterized by what I would describe as emotional excess. There is nothing, for example, to match the barking, the speaking in tongues, the "powerful convulsions" which characterized the nineteenth-century McDonaldite revivals on Prince Edward Island. All these phenomena were regarded by the Baptists as being "very wild"[50] and to be avoided at all costs. And well-ordered revivals, as a consequence, have become the Nova Scotia Baptist norm. Nova Scotia conservatism thus triumphed over Yankee enthusiasm.

The Reverend Isaiah Wallace's career, as probably the best-known Baptist evangelist in Nova Scotia and New Brunswick in the latter half of the nineteenth century, serves to underscore the accuracy of this conclusion. In the 1850s in New Brunswick, but not Nova Scotia, Wallace noted that the

Spirits mighty power in subduing the hearts of men was wonderful. . . . the meetings were sometimes noisy and full of excitement and being comparatively inexperienced, I found it necessary in presiding in the services to seek continually God's steadying hand.[51]

Never again in his descriptions of the many revivals in which he was intimately involved between 1860 and 1900, would Wallace ever use the word "noisy." Evidently the "steadying hand" was ever present, especially in Nova Scotia, to ensure, as he put it "this blessed work" would be both "ordered" and "respectable."

VI

In Nova Scotia, according to a public opinion survey conducted in 1977 by the Task Force on Canadian Unity, only 7 percent of the Baptist respondents had ever been positively affected by a religious revival and a little more than 2 percent by the charismatic movement. In New Brunswick, on the other hand, 25 percent of the Baptists had been positively affected by a religious revival and only 1 percent by the charismatic movement. As far as the non-Baptist population in Nova Scotia was concerned, the corresponding percentages were 5 percent and 1 percent and in New Brunswick 7 percent and 3.5 percent.

The evidence suggests that the Nova Scotia Baptist revivalist tradition – unlike that of New Brunswick – may have lost much of its hold on the denomination's ethos. It is a historical tradition of central importance but also apparently a contemporary reality of growing insignificance. It is of some consequence, I think, that only approximately 11 percent of all Nova Scotia Baptists regard themselves as being either "high" or "medium high" in the area of perceived religiosity. And almost two out of three of the Nova Scotia Baptists consider themselves as being either "non-religious" or "very low." In New Brunswick, only two in five Baptists locate themselves in these categories. If this secularization trend continues – a trend confirmed by 1981 census data – by 1991 almost three in four Nova Scotia Baptists will, in fact, be virtual non-believers, as will one in two of New Brunswick Baptists. Obviously, the denomination faces serious problems in the immediate future, despite the much heralded neo-evangelical revival. [52]

But is it necessarily that inevitable? Is there something especially irreversible about the secularization process? Social trends can always be checked or even turned around. And consequently the next few decades in Nova Scotia and New Brunswick may see the Whig forces of progress and change switched back on to themselves by the unexpected and the unanticipated realities of late twentieth-century existence.

As far as Henry Alline was concerned, the problems facing his Nova Scotia in 1775 were far more distressing and far more disturbing than those impinging on the province in the spring of 1984. He found solace and inspiration in what became one of his favourite texts – the first three verses of the 40th Psalm.

1. I waited patiently for the Lord; and he inclined unto me, and heard my cry.
2. He brought me up also out of the horrible pit, out of the miry clay, and set my feet upon a rock, and established my goings.
3. And he hath put a new song in my mouth, even praise unto our God: many see it, and fear, and shall trust in the Lord.

A few months before he died Alline wrote to a friend, William Wells,

Altho the Carnal world & dry Pharisee will account all pretensions to a felt knowledge of Christ, & the Joys of the Holy Ghost as vain. Yet it is the only Joy & Life of my Soul . . . in these Trying hours when Earthly friends, Comforts Joys and all Created helpers prove abortive. Ah When all things else shall fail Jesus is a friend and Supporter, Comforter, & Everlasting portion & reward. I have been sometimes so weak in body I could Scarcely Speak, & my Soul could mount up & Rejoice. Jesus made me Strong In His Grace.

O William, it is a Religion that the world despises But it is Joy unspeakable & Life Eternal to the Despised followers of Jesus.[53]

Despite everything, there is still hope for the "Despised followers of Jesus" – Henry Alline and his disciples certainly knew why.

Notes

NOTES TO CHAPTER 1

1 For biographical information concerning Alline, see J.M. Bumsted, *Henry Alline* (Toronto, 1971) and G. Stewart and G.A. Rawlyk, *A People Highly Favoured of God: The Nova Scotia Yankees and the American Revolution* (Toronto 1972).

2 For a recent sensitive study of Alline as a hymn writer, see Margaret A. Filshie, "Redeeming Love Shall Be Our Song,' Hymns of the First Great Awakening in Nova Scotia," (M.A. thesis, Queen's University, 1983).

3 J. More, *The History of Queens County, Nova Scotia* (Halifax, N.S., 1873), p. 162.

4 See J. Davis, *Life and Times of the Late Rev. Harris Harding, Yarmouth, N.S.* (Charlottetown, P.E.I., 1866), p. 178.

5 (New York, 1916), pp. 159, 217.

6 H. Alline, *The Life and Journal* (Boston, 1806), pp. 26 – 7. Throughout this volume I have used the 1806 *Journal* version rather than the J. Beverley and B. Moody (ed.) *The Journal of Henry Alline* (Hantsport, N.S., 1982).

7 Alline, *Life and Journal*, p. 34.

8 Ibid., pp. 34 – 5.

9 Ibid., p. 35.

10 The crucial importance of the "New Birth" in the New Light tradition in New England's First Great Awakening is suggested in A. Heimert, *Religion and the American Mind* (Cambridge, Mass., 1966).

11 H. Alline, *Two Mites: Some of the Most Important and much disputed Points of Divinity* (Halifax, N.S., 1781), pp. 150 – 1. Hereafter, *Two Mites* (Halifax, N.S., 1893).

12 H. Alline, *The Anti-Traditionalist* (Halifax, N.S., 1983) pp. 53 – 4.

13 S.A. Marini, "New England Folk Religions 1770 – 1815: The Sectarian Impulse in Revolutionary Society" (Ph.d. thesis, Harvard Divinity School, 1978), p. 20. Professor Marini's dissertation, in much revised form, has been recently published under the title *Radical Sects of Revolutionary New England* (Cambridge, Mass., 1982).

14 M. Richey, *A Memoir of the Late Rev. William Black* (Halifax, N.S., 1839), p. 45.

15 I have developed this theme at somewhat greater length in "Nova Scotia and the American Revolution," in O.D. Edwards and G. Shepperson (eds.), *Scotland, Europe and the American Revolution* (Edinburgh, 1976), pp. 104 – 10.

16 This theme is developed in G.A. Rawlyk and Gordon Stewart, "Nova Scotia's Sense of Mission," *Social History* (November 1968): 5 – 17.

17 Alline, *Two Mites*, p. 274.

18 *Christian Instructor and Missionary Register of the Presbyterian Church of Nova Scotia* (March 1859). For a further discussion of some of the non-Biblical influences on Alline's theology and imagery, see Stewart and Rawlyk, *A People Highly Favoured of God*, p. 82 – 5.

19 Alline, *Life and Journal*, p. 17.

20 Ibid., p. 180. A more detailed consideration of the importance of the manuscript journal is to be found in my *New Light Letters and Songs* (Hantsport, N.S., 1983), pp. 8 – 9.

21 See, for example, Professor Stewart's critical comments concerning Alline's *Journal* in his review of Beverley and Moody, *The Journal of Henry Alline* in *The Canadian Historical Review*, vol. 64, no. 2 (June 1983): 240 – 1.

22 Alline, *Life and Journal*, p. 35.

23 Ibid.

24 Ibid.

25 Ibid., pp. 35 – 6.

26 Ibid., p. 36.

27 Ibid., pp. 36 – 7.

28 Ibid.
29 Ibid., pp. 34 – 5.
30 Ibid., pp. 36 – 8.
31 E. Erikson, *Young Man Luther* (New York, 1958), p. 41.
32 E. Erikson, *Identity, Youth and Crisis* (New York 1968), pp. 22 – 3.
33 See B. Bailyn, *The Ideological Origins of the American Revolution* (Cambridge, Mass., 1967).
34 M. Armstrong, "Neutrality and Religion in Revolutionary Nova Scotia," in G.A. Rawlyk (ed.), *Historical Essays on the Atlantic Provinces* (Toronto, 1967), p. 40.
35 Alline, *Life and Journal*, pp. 38 – 9.
36 Ibid., pp. 39 – 41.
37 Ibid., pp. 41 – 2.
38 Ibid., pp. 42 – 3.
39 Ibid., p. 44.
40 Ibid.
41 All the quotations in this paragraph are from ibid., pp. 46 – 8.
42 Ibid., p. 47.
43 Ibid., p. 48.
44 Ibid., p. 54.
45 Ibid., pp. 56 – 7.
46 Ibid., p. 59.
47 All the quotations in this paragraph are from ibid., pp. 61 – 2.
48 Ibid., p. 68.
49 Ibid., p. 70.
50 Ibid., pp. 71 – 3.
51 Ibid., pp. 73 – 4.
52 All the quotations in this paragraph are from ibid., pp. 75 – 8.
53 Ibid., pp. 78 – 82.
54 Ibid., pp. 82 – 9.
55 Ibid., p. 85.
56 Ibid., p. 93.
57 Ibid., pp. 97 – 9.
58 Ibid., p. 103.
59 Ibid., pp. 105 – 36.

60 Peter Shaw, *American Patriots and the Rituals of Revolution* (Cambridge, Mass., 1981), p. 165. See also E.D. Witthower, "Psychological Aspects of Polmonary Tuberculosis: A General Survey," in P.J. Sparer (ed.), *Personality Stress and Tuberculosis* (New York, 1956), p. 157 – 8.

61 Alline, *Life and Journal*, p. 131.

62 Ibid., p. 131 – 3.

63 Ibid., p. 136.

64 Ibid., p. 140.

65 Ibid., p. 143.

66 Ibid.

67 Ibid., p. 144.

68 Ibid.

69 Ibid., p. 145.

70 Ibid., pp. 146 – 9. *See also* Stewart and Rawlyk, *A People Highly Favoured of God*, pp. 98 – 139 and Gordon Stewart (ed.), *The Great Awakening in Nova Scotia* (Toronto, 1982). The point should be emphatically made that when Alline's accounts of his visits to various regions of Nova Scotia are carefully checked with other contemporary accounts, Alline is seen to have been an accurate, fair, and perceptive observer. If anything, he seems to have underestimated his influence.

71 Alline, *Life and Journal*, pp. 149 – 53.

72 All the quotations in this paragraph are from ibid., pp. 153 – 64.

73 All the quotations in this paragraph are from ibid., pp. 165 – 7.

74 All the quotations in this paragraph are from ibid., pp. 168 – 70.

75 Ibid., p. 171.

76 Ibid., p. 172 – 3.

NOTES TO CHAPTER 2

1 See S.A. Marini, *Radical Sects of Revolutionary New England* (Cambridge, Mass., 1982). In his book, unlike in his Ph.D. dissertation, Professor Marini stresses the importance of Nova Scotia's Great Awakening in helping to bring about the "New Light Stir." Throughout this chapter I will refer both to his thesis and to his book.

2 Alline, *The Life and Journal* (Boston, 1806), p. 173.

3 Ibid., p. 174.

4 Ibid., p. 176.

5 Ibid., pp. 178 – 9.

6 See ibid., pp. 30 – 9.

7 Ibid., p. 180.

8 Ibid.

9 North Hampton Congregational Church Book, New Hampshire Historical Society, Concord, N.H.

10 See, for example, *Christian Instructor and Missionary Register of the Presbyterian Church of Nova Scotia* (March 1859).

11 See S.A. Marini, "New England Folk Religions 1770 – 1815: The Sectarian Impulse in Revolutionary Society" (Ph.d thesis, Harvard Divinity School, 1978), p. 54.

12 Ibid., p. 71.

13 John Buzzell, *The Life of Elder Benjamin Randel, Principally Taken from Documents Written by Himself* (Limerick, Ma., 1827), p. 12.

14 Ibid., p. 13.

15 N.A. Baxter, *History of the Freewill Baptists* (Rochester, N.Y., 1957), p. 5.

16 Buzzell, *Randel*, p. 20 – 1.

17 Ibid., p. 21.

18 Marini, "New England Folk Religions," p. 78.

19 Ibid., p. 80.

20 Ibid., p. 86.

21 Ibid., p. 96. See also Marini, *Radical Sects*, pp. 40 – 59.

22 G.P. Murdock, "Ethnographic Atlas: A Summary," *Ethnology* vol. 1, no. 2 (April 1967): 112.

23 Marini, *Radical Sects*, p. 47.

24 Quoted in Marini, "New England Folk Religions," p. 104.

25 Ibid., p. 107.

26 For a discussion of other perfectionist sects, see Marini, *Radical Sects*, p. 51.

27 H.D. McLennan, *History of Gorham, Maine* (Portland, Me., 1903), p. 201.

28 Ibid., p. 204.

29 See the Church Records of the Cornwallis and Horton Baptist Church in the Acadia University Archives.

30 Marini, "New England Folk Religions," p. 119.
31 Buzzell, *Randel*, pp. 87 – 8.
32 All the quotations in this paragraph are from ibid., pp. 88 – 9.
33 Ibid., p. 89.
34 Ibid.
35 Marini, "New England Folk Religions," pp. 184, 188.
36 Ibid., p. 191.
37 Ibid., p. 109.
38 Buzzell, *Randel*, pp. 84 – 5.
39 I.D. Stewart, *History of the Freewill Baptists* (Dover, N.H., 1862), p. 75.
40 Ibid.
41 Ibid., p. 55.
42 Baxter, *History of the Freewill Baptists*, p. 55.
43 Buzzell, *Randel*, p. 115.
44 Ibid., p. 116.
45 Stewart, *History of the Freewill Baptists*, p. 81.
46 See M. Armstrong, *The Great Awakening in Nova Scotia 1776 – 1809* (Hartford, Conn., 1948), p. 91. See also M. Filshie, " 'Redeeming Love Shall Be Our Song:' Hymns of the First Great Awakening in Nova Scotia" (M.A. thesis, Queen's University, 1983) and T.B. Vincent "Some Bibliographic Notes on Henry Alline's *Hymns and Spiritual Songs*," *Canadian Notes and Queries* (November 1973): 12 – 3 and G.A. Rawlyk "Henry Alline and the Canadian Baptist Tradition," *Theological Bulletin*, McMaster Divinity College (1977).
47 Armstrong, *The Great Awakening in Nova Scotia*, p. 91.
48 Stewart, *History of the Freewill Baptists*, p. 80.
49 Armstrong, *The Great Awakening in Nova Scotia*, p. 92.
50 Rev. J. Scott, *Brief View* (Halifax, 1784), p. 168.
51 Armstrong, *The Great Awakening in Nova Scotia*, p. 91.
52 Ibid., p. 92.
53 Baxter, *History of the Freewill Baptists*, p. 55. Baxter's study was originally a Harvard Divinity School Ph.d. thesis completed in 1954.
54 Ibid., p. 56.
55 Ibid.
56 Ibid.

57 Ibid., pp. 57 – 9.
58 Marini, "New England Folk Religions," p. 347; Marini, *Radical Sects*, p. 139.
59 Marini, "New England Folk Religions," pp. 347 – 8.
60 Ibid., pp. 354 – 62; Marini, *Radical Sects*, pp. 139 – 44.
61 Randel, *Sermon*, p. 6.
62 Ibid., p. 8.
63 Marini, "New England Folk Religions," p. 357.
64 Ibid., pp. 358 – 9.
65 Randel, *Sermon*, pp. 7 – 13.
66 Ibid., pp. 13 – 5.
67 Marini, "New England Folk Religions," pp. 450 – 1. See also Marini, *Radical Sects*, pp. 158 – 62.
68 Marini, "New England Folk Religions," p. 452.
69 J. Buzzell, *Psalms, Hymns, and Spiritual Songs* (Dover, N.H., 1823), pp. 257 – 9.
70 Alline, *Hymns and Spiritual Songs*, p. 348.
71 Marini, *Radical Sects*, p. 170 – 1.
72 Marini, "New England Folk Religions," pp. 480 – 1.
73 Ibid., p. 482.
74 For a more detailed discussion of this issue, see D. Stratas, "A Study of the Historical Demography of the Maritime Provinces, 1763 – 1901" (Unpublished paper, Department of History, Queen's University, 1981).
75 Marini, "New England Folk Religions," p. 2.
76 Ibid., p. 349.
77 This theme is developed in D.D. Bruce Jr., *And They All Sang Hallelujah: Plain-Folk Camp Meeting Religion 1800 – 1845* (Knoxville, Tenn., 1974), p. 95.
78 *Christian Instructor and Missionary Register of the Presbyterian Church of Nova Scotia* (February 1859).

NOTES TO CHAPTER 3

1 *Christian Instructor and Missionary Register of the Presbyterian Church of Nova Scotia* (March 1859).

144 / Notes to pp 73-82

2 J. Davis, *Life and Times of the Late Reverend Harris Harding, Yarmouth, N.S.* (Charlottetown, P.E.I., 1866), p. 187.

3 Ibid.

4 Quoted in M. Armstrong, *The Great Awakening in Nova Scotia 1776 – 1809* (Hartford, Conn., 1948), p. 86.

5 Public Archives of Nova Scotia. (Hereafter PANS.) "Mathew Byles III Journal," MG 1 vol. 163.

6 PANS. "Records of the Church of Jeboque in Yarmouth," p. 138.

7 Ibid., p. 140.

8 S.A. Marini, "New England Folk Religions 1770 – 1815: The Sectarian Impulse in Revolutionary Society" (Ph.d. thesis, Harvard Divinity School, 1978), p. 2.

9 M. Richey, *A Memoir of the Late Rev. William Black* (Halifax, N.S.), p. 45.

10 Quoted in Marini, "New England Folk Religions," pp. 453 – 4.

11 D.C. Harvey (ed.), *Diary of Simeon Perkins, 1780 – 1789* (Toronto, 1958), p. 177.

12 See for example, H. Alline, *The Anti-Traditionalist* (Halifax, N.S., 1783), p. 36.

13 Ibid., p. 40.

14 PANS. M.G. 1 no. 100, pp. 428 – 31.

15 See, for example, N. MacKinnon, "The Loyalist Experience in Nova Scotia 1783 – 1791" (Ph.d. thesis, Queen's University, 1974).

16 G. Wood, "Evangelical America and Early Mormonism" (paper presented to the 15th annual meeting of the Mormon History Association, May 1980), p. 2.

17 Quoted in J.M Cramp, "History of the Maritime Baptists" (Acadia University Archives), p. 26.

18 Wood, "Evangelical America," p. 7.

19 Ibid., p. 12.

20 This theme is developed at much greater length in my *New Light Letters and Songs* (Hantsport, N.S., 1983), pp. 4 – 66, 316 – 25. Some of the documented "grave Antinomian excesses" involved fornication, adultery, and religious practices such as women riding on the backs of men.

21 B.C. Cuthbertson (ed.), *The Journal of John Payzant* (Hantsport, N.S., 1981), pp. 43 – 8.

22 United Church Archives, Toronto, "Freeborn Garrettson Journal." See also Rawlyk, *New Light Letters and Songs*, pp. 48 – 9, 56 – 9, 148, 339 – 41.

23 Cuthbertson, *The Journal of John Payzant*, p. 44.

24 Rawlyk, *New Light Letters and Songs*, pp. 58 – 63.

25 C.B. Fergusson (ed.), *Perkin's Diary, 1797 – 1803* (Toronto, 1967), p. 45.

26 See my discussion of Harris Harding, in "From New Light to Baptist: Harris Harding and the Second Great Awakening in Nova Scotia," in B. Moody (ed.), *Repent and Believe* (Hantsport, N.S., 1980), pp. 1 – 26.

27 Quoted in Cramp, "History of the Maritime Baptists," p. 24.

28 New Dispensation-like movements were fairly common in northern New England at the same time. See S.A. Marini, *Radical Sects of Revolutionary New England* (Cambridge, Mass., 1982) for a good overview of what I would describe as the fragmenting evangelical ethos.

29 Davis, *Harris Harding*, p. 184.

30 Ibid., p. 185.

31 Ibid., p. 184.

32 Ibid.

33 See "The Manning Journal" for the 1820s in the Acadia University Archives. In this remarkable journal is to be found an often introspective account of one man's torturous spiritual and intellectual journey from Alline's Free-Will New Lightism to Scott's eighteenth-century Calvinist orthodoxy.

34 See E.C. Wright, "Without Intervention of Prophet, Priest or King," in Moody, *Repent and Believe*, p. 70.

35 See A. Robertson, " 'Draughts of Wormwood and Gall' The Antinomian Challenge in Eighteenth Century Nova Scotia" (Unpublished paper, Wolfville, N.S., 1983), pp. 32 – 3.

36 See Rawlyk, "From New Light to Baptist," in Moody, *Repent and Believe*, pp. 20 – 1. For a somewhat different interpretation of the professionalization of the ministry, see D.M. Scott, *From Office to Profession: The New England Ministry 1750 – 1850* (Philadelphia, 1978).

37 Quoted in *Classified Digest of the Records of the Society for the Propagation of the Gospel in Foreign Parts, 1701 – 1892* (London, 1983), p. 118.

38 Quoted in E.M. Saunders, *History of the Baptists of the Maritime Provinces* (Halifax, N.S., 1902), p. 115.

39 Ibid.

40 Cramp, "History of the Maritime Baptists," pp. 74 – 5.
41 Quoted in ibid., p. 75.
42 Ibid.
43 Cuthbertson, *The Journal of John Payzant,* p. 79.
44 Ibid.
45 Quoted in Cramp, "History of the Maritime Baptists," p. 75.
46 Ibid., p. 76.
47 Ibid.
48 See Rawlyk, "From New Light to Baptist," in Moody, *Repent and Believe,* pp. 24 – 5.
49 See Rawlyk, "Nova Scotia and New Brunswick Number of Baptists and Percentage of Population, 1827 – 1981" (Unpublished paper, Kingston, 1983).
50 Innis Diary, Acadia University Archives.
51 Thomas Griffin to Edward Manning, 12 September 1818, Manning Letters, Acadia University Archives.
52 Ibid., 5 November 1818.
53 Manning Journal, Acadia University Archives.
54 Ibid.
55 E. Reis to Edward Manning, 16 April 1817, Manning Letters, Acadia University Archives.
56 Ibid., 18 April 1817.
57 See Professor Barry Moody's important study "From Itinerant to Settled Pastor: The Case of Edward Manning," a paper read before the Canadian Society of Church History, Halifax, N.S., June 1981.
58 For further background material, consult P.G.A. Allwood, "Joseph Howe is Their Devil: Controversies among Regular Baptists in Halifax, 1827 – 1868," in Moody, *Repent and Believe,* pp. 76 – 7.
59 Ibid., p. 83.
60 B. Moody, "The Maritime Baptists and Higher Education in the Early Nineteenth Century," ibid., p. 98.
61 See J.M. Beck, *Joseph Howe Conservative Reformer 1804 – 1848* (vol. 1) (Kingston, 1982), pp. 248 – 55, 257 – 65.
62 Ibid., p. 259.
63 Ibid., pp. 259 – 62.

64 E. Smith, *The Life, Conversion, Preaching, Travels and Sufferings of Elias Smith* (Portsmouth, N.H., 1816), pp. 280, 324.

65 This description of the "Babcock Tragedy" is based on the account to be found in the *New Brunswick Magazine* (October 1898), pp. 214 – 22.

66 Quoted in ibid., pp. 221 – 22.

67 Undated autobiographical fragment, Manning Letters, Acadia University Archives.

68 See G.A. Rawlyk, "From New Light to Baptist," in Moody, *Repent and Believe*, p. 8.

69 S. Marini, *Radical Sects of Revolutionary New England* (Cambridge, Mass., 1982), pp. 172 – 6.

70 Smith, *The Life, Conversion . . .*, pp. 300 – 1.

71 Mr. David Bell of Fredericton, New Brunswick is doing important research in this area and when his findings are published they will, I am sure, significantly revise our understanding of evangelical religion in early nineteenth-century New Brunswick.

72 See J.L Thomas, "Romantic Reform in America, 1815 – 1865," *American Quarterly* 17 (Winter, 1965): 658 – 59. For a similar response to that of the Maritime evangelicals, see A.C. Loveland, *Southern Evangelicals and the Social Order* (Baton Rouge, La., 1980).

73 H. Alline, *Two Mites* (Halifax, N.S., 1781), pp. 19 – 20.

NOTES TO CHAPTER 4

1 The Wallace "revitalization thesis" forms the core of W.G. McLoughlin's suggestive *Revivals, Awakenings and Reform* (Chicago, 1978). Some of the themes developed in this chapter are to be found in my "New Lights, Baptists and Religious Awakenings in Nova Scotia 1776 – 1843: A Preliminary Probe," *Journal* of the Church Historical Society, vol. 25, no. 2 (October 1983): 43 – 73.

2 I have attempted to develop this argument in my *The Atlantic Provinces and the Problems of Confederation* (St. John's, Nfld., 1979).

3 This book, together with Stephen Marini's *Radical Sects of Revolutionary New England* (Cambridge, Mass., 1983) and Donald Mathews' *Religion*

in the Old South (Chicago, 1977), have significantly influenced my view of Maritime revivals and Maritime revivalism.

4 See his important and cogently argued article "American Culture and the English-Canadian Mind at the End of the Nineteenth Century," *Journal of Popular Culture*, vol. 4 (Spring, 1971): 1050.

5 H. Alline, *Life and Journal* (Boston, 1806), p. 167.

6 Ibid.

7 See Rev. J. Scott, *Brief View* (Halifax, 1784), pp. 163, 227.

8 Alline, *Life and Journal*, p. 174.

9 Quoted in J.M. Cramp, "History of the Maritime Baptists" (Acadia University Archives), p. 49.

10 For an excellent description of the New Light exhorter at work, see G.E. Levy (ed.), *The Diary of Joseph Dimock* (Hantsport, N.S., 1979), pp. 23 – 6 and pp. 30 – 8, in particular.

11 All of the quotations in this paragraph are in the Nancy Lawrence De Wolfe letters, to be found in my *New Light Letters and Songs* (Hantsport, N.S., 1983), pp. 353 – 4.

12 See B.C. Cuthbertson (ed.), *The Journal of John Payzant* (Hantsport, N.S., 1981), pp. 85 – 9 for all of the quotations in this paragraph concerning the Liverpool revival.

13 V. Turner, *The Ritual Process: Structure and Anti-Structure* (Ithaca, N.Y., 1979), p. 138.

14 "The Journal of Henry Hale," Maine State Archives and the "Isaac Case Diary," Colby College Archives.

15 E. Smith, *The Life, Conversion, Preaching, Travels and Sufferings of Elias Smith* (Portsmouth, N.H., 1816), p. 280.

16 See Cuthbertson, *Payzant Journal*, p. 79.

17 See the "James Innis Journal," Acadia University Archives.

18 Ibid.

19 I am now developing this theme in an article entitled "Henry Hale, Isaac Case, Daniel Merrill and the New Brunswick and Nova Scotia Baptists, 1805 to 1812."

20 See his *Ritual Process* (especially pp. 94 – 140). The quotations in this paragraph are from this section of Turner's suggestive volume.

21 The quotations in this paragraph are from ibid., pp. 139 – 40.

22 See my *New Light Letters and Songs* (Hantsport, N.S., 1983), pp. 36 – 66 and my "From New Light to Baptist: Harris Harding and the Second Great Awakening in Nova Scotia," in B. Moody (ed.), *Repent and Believe* (Hantsport, N.S., 1980), pp. 1 – 26.

23 (1808), pp. 303 – 5.

24 See his often evocative description of the "reformation" in Cuthbertson (ed.), *Payzant Journal*, pp. 85 – 90.

25 Ibid., p. 89.

26 Ibid., p. 90.

27 This section dealing with Nancy Lawrence De Wolf is based upon her letters to be found in the American Antiquarian Society, Worcester, Massachusetts. See Rawlyk, *New Light Letters*, pp. 276 – 8.

28 Nancy De Wolf to her mother, 5 January 1791, American Antiquarian Society.

29 Ibid.

30 See the three letters in the American Antiquarian Society, Worcester, Mass.

31 The quotations are from the letters to be found in Rawlyk, *New Light Letters*, pp. 352 – 3.

32 Ibid., pp. 353 – 4.

33 Ibid., p. 355.

34 For a similar phenomenon, see P. Boyer and S. Nissenbaum, *Salem Possessed* (Cambridge, 1974), p. 28 – 9. See also Turner, *The Ritual Process*, pp. 166 – 203.

35 Harris Harding to Mr. and Mrs. Young, 10 May 1828, quoted in Cramp, "History of the Maritime Baptists," p. 173.

36 This paragraph and the one which follows is based upon D. Mathews, *Religion in the American South* (Chicago, 1977), pp. 40, 105 – 10.

37 Ibid., p. 105.

38 Ibid.

39 J. Rand to D. Freeman, 22 December 1859, Manning Letters, vol. 9, Acadia University Archives.

40 Mathews, *Religion in the Old South*, p. 105.

41 See A. Wallace, "Revitalization Movements," *American Anthropology*, vol. 58 (1956): 264 – 81.

42 Quoted in McLoughlin, *Revivals*, p. 125.

43 Harris Harding is a good example of this. See, for example, my "From New Light to Baptist," p. 126.
44 "The Intellectual Awakening of Nova Scotia," *Dalhousie Review* 13 (April 1933): 1 – 22.
45 Quoted in Cramp, History of the Maritime Baptists," p. 186.
46 Quoted in ibid., p. 190.
47 Quoted in ibid., p. 191.
48 "Manning Journal, 24 August 1821," Acadia University Archives.
49 Ibid., 10 September 1821.
50 Samuel McCulley to Edward Manning, 18 November 1830, Acadia University Archives. See also David Weale, "The Ministry of the Reverend Donald McDonald on Prince Edward Island 1826 – 1867: A Case-Study Examination of the Influence and Role of Religion Within Colonial Society" (Ph.d. thesis, Queen's University, 1976), pp. 107 – 16. These "convulsive effects" were referred to by friends and enemies alike as "the works."
51 I. Wallace, *Autobiographical Sketch with Reminiscences of Revival Work* (Halifax, n.d.,) p. 23.
52 See the Task Force on Canadian Unity Survey Data, to be found at Queen's University, Kingston, Ontario.
53 Quoted in Rawlyk, *New Light Letters and Songs,* p. 85.

Appendix A

Nova Scotia and New Brunswick Baptists:
Some Similarities and Some Differences

A Preliminary Probe

Late in 1977, I began a study on the Atlantic provinces and the problems of Confederation for the Task Force on Canadian Unity. One of the projects invoved a large-scale public opinion survey in the region. This survey was organized and implemented by Professor George Perlin, of the Political Studies Department, Queen's University, with whom I was associated in the project. I was able to insert a few questions about religion in the survey, hoping thereby to answer some of my questions about the continuing impact evangelical Christianity might be having on Nova Scotia and New Brunswick, in particular, and on the Atlantic region in general. There were 855 Nova Scotians included in the weighted sample and 695 New Brunswickers, out of a total sample of 2,183. Questions 91, 92, 93, and 94 related specifically to religious matters and dealt with perceived religiosity, involvement in religious revivals or the charismatic movement, witnessing for one's faith, and involvement in one's church.

A denominational breakdown, taking into account these four questions, has been carried out. Data concerning the five major denominations, the Roman Catholic, United, Anglican, Baptist, and Presbyterian Churches have been included for Nova Scotia; members of these denominations, it should be pointed out, make up almost 88 percent of the Nova Scotia population.

Nova Scotia	Roman Catholic	United Church	Anglican	Presby-terian	Baptist
	(percent)	(percent)	(percent)	(percent)	(percent)
Highly Religious	1.0	2.6	1.1	0.0	6.2
Medium High	5.1	4.3	2.3	7.3	4.6
Medium Low	29.9	31.0	25.0	29.3	24.6
Low	36.5	38.8	38.6	39.0	29.2
Non-Religious	27.5	23.3	33.0	24.4	35.4

It is noteworthy that 10.8 percent of the Nova Scotia Baptist sample regarded themselves as being "highly religious" or "medium high," in comparison with 6.1 percent of the Roman Catholics, 6.9 percent of the United Church members, and 3.4 percent of the Anglicans. And, furthermore, at the opposite end of the scale, 35.4 percent of the

Baptists described themselves as being "non-religious" – while only 27.5 percent of the Roman Catholics categorized themselves in this manner, and 23.3 percent of United Church adherents, 33.0 percent of the Anglicans, and 24.4 percent of the relatively small Presbyterian population.

In neighbouring New Brunswick, the data confirms impressionistic and historical studies which have suggested that New Brunswick religious culture, in general, and the Baptists in particular, are more conservative and more "evangelical" than their Nova Scotia counterparts. This grass roots reality may help to explain some of the tensions which have divided the Maritime Baptist Convention in recent years along Nova Scotia and New Brunswick lines. Roman Catholics, Anglicans, Baptists, and United Church members and adherents make up close to 90 percent of New Brunswick's total population and are therefore the only denominations included in the following table.

(New Brunswick)	Roman Catholic	United Church	Anglican	Baptist
	(percent)	(percent)	(percent)	(percent)
Highly Religious	3.3	1.1	2.7	8.6
Medium High	10.8	13.6	5.5	18.5
Medium Low	30.2	27.3	24.7	30.9
Low	39.6	37.5	41.1	23.5
Non-Religious	16.1	20.5	26.0	18.5

What is particularly striking in a comparison of the two tables is the fact that only a little more than 10 percent of Nova Scotia Baptists consider themselves to be "highly religious" or "medium high" as compared to 27 percent of the New Brunswick Baptists. Moreover, at the opposite end of the scale, almost two in three Nova Scotia Baptists regard themselves as being "non-religious" or "low," compared to two out of five New Brunswick Baptists. These figures, let me emphasize, merely reflect trends and these trends, of course, were perceived in 1978.

There is yet another way to note certain differences between Nova Scotia and New Brunswick Baptists. It is clear, for example, that the

Free Will tradition was far more important in New Brunswick than in Nova Scotia. In 1871, it should be noted, out of a total New Brunswick population of 285,594 (33.6 percent of which was Roman Catholic) there were 42,729 "Regular Baptists" – 15 percent of the population, and 27,866 Free Will Baptists – 9.8 percent of the total population. In Nova Scotia in 1871, out of a total population of 387,800 (26.5 percent of which was Roman Catholic) there were only 19,032 Free Will Baptists (4.9 percent of the total population and 54,263 Regular Baptists (14.0 percent of the total population). In 1881, the New Brunswick Regular Baptists made up 15.4 percent of the total population, and the Free Will Baptists 9.8 percent, while in Nova Scotia, the Regular Baptists made up 16.6 percent and the Free Will Baptists 2.4 percent. By 1891, in New Brunswick, the Free Will Baptists had dropped to 7.7 percent, and a decade later to 4.7 percent, while the Regular Baptists increased to 17.1 percent, and then to 19.7 percent. In Nova Scotia, by 1891, the Free Will Baptists had fallen to 2.3 percent and a decade later to 1.8 percent.

It may be argued that at the beginning of the twentieth century, during the decade when the two Baptist groups officially merged, approximately 40 percent of all New Brunswick Baptists came from the Free Will Baptist tradition. But in Nova Scotia, only 25 percent of the approximately 75,000 Baptists did so. And the Free Will Baptist tradition had at its core far more than what has often been referred to as a "Free Grace Arminianism." There was also a radically different way of perceiving worship and church polity. Many would maintain that the Free Will Baptists were, in certain key respects, the real disciples of Henry Alline, and the truly committed transmitters of the New Light Gospel.

And as has been alluded to earlier, the similarities and differences between New Brunswick and Nova Scotia Baptists should be viewed not only in the religious, but also within the secular, context. Religion, of course, cannot be looked at in splendid isolation, for it is only one important indicator of the cultural ethos of a region. It should always be kept in mind that in the eighteenth, nineteenth, and twentieth centuries, New Brunswick's historical development, broadly defined, was quite different from Nova Scotia's. For example, the Loyalists had a far greater impact on the life of New Brunswick than they did on Nova Scotia, where the Yankee influence was far more important. In Nova Scotia, furthermore, the Scots were of greater consequence than in New Brunswick. In New Brunswick, from the American Revolution to the present, the Acadians and Irish have been far more important than in Nova Scotia. The point is, that despite their similarities, despite the many Maritime and regional characteristics they obviously have shared, and do share, Nova Scotia is different from New Brunswick. And these historical, cultural, demographic, and economic differences, as well as the similarities, provide the backdrop for any examination of the religious life of the two provinces. This is such an obvious point that it is sometimes forgotten.

There is yet another way to try to come to grips with the problems of possible similarities and differences between New Brunswick and Nova Scotia Baptists. The way is not usually travelled by the historian or by the theologian but rather by the political scientist and by the sociologist. And this brings me back to the first few pages of this appendix – back to the 1978 Task Force on Canadian Unity public opinion survey.

The survey data, I have found, can be used to discover a great deal of information about the views and attitudes of Nova Scotia and New Brunswick Baptists concerning a myriad of issues. And they show how much New Brunswick and Nova Scotia Baptists actually have in common and where, especially in the area of Anglo-French relations and perceived religiosity, they may differ. In a very real sense the public opinion survey data appear to confirm the somewhat impressionistic conclusions of a few recent scholars. But far more research into the past and into the contemporary Baptist mind will have to be done before these impressions – however enlightened – are definitively confirmed.

Though the actual New Brunswick and Nova Scotia Baptist sample size was relatively small, fewer than 100 in both cases, the mathematically computed margin of error, with respect to the Baptist sample, was not unreasonable. In fact, statistical theory suggests that the Baptist percentages are accurate within 9.9 percentage points, nineteen times out of twenty. The margin of error for the non-Baptist sample, of course, is much lower – lower, in fact, than the 4 percent of the Gallup poll.

Task Force on Canadian Unity
Public Opinion Survey, 1978

	New Brunswick			Nova Scotia	
	Non Baptist	Baptist	Franco-phones	Non Baptists	Baptists
Q 1. How do you think of yourself first?					
	(percent)	(percent)	(percent)	(percent)	(percent)
Canadian	62	63	50	60	57
Maritimer	10	13	7	7	3
New Brunswicker	20	11	33	21	30
Other	8	13	10	12	10
Q 5a. In terms of your personal feelings towards them, do you feel closer to people in					
	(percent)	(percent)	(percent)	(percent)	(percent)
New England	33	35	27	34	42
Ontario	57	55	56	58	46
Equally Close	9	9	8	7	10
Neither	1	1	9	1	2
Q 5b. Do you feel closer to people in					
	(percent)	(percent)	(percent)	(percent)	(percent)
Quebec	49	15	72	42	19
New England	43	74	15	52	71
Equally Close	7	10	7	5	8
Neither	1	1	6	1	2
Q 5c. Do you feel closer to people in					
	(percent)	(percent)	(percent)	(percent)	(percent)
Ontario	64	59	72	57	59
West	22	25	7	34	24
Equally Close	13	14	10	9	14
Neither	1	2	11	0	2

		New Brunswick			Nova Scotia	
		Non Baptist	Baptist	Franco-phones	Non Baptists	Baptists
Q 5d.	Do you feel closer to people in					
		(percent)	(percent)	(percent)	(percent)	(percent)
West		41	75	12	58	63
Quebec		48	7	74	34	24
Equally Close		10	6	6	8	10
Neither		1	12	8	0	3

Q 7f.   Generally speaking, what is your opinion of Upper Canadians?

	(percent)	(percent)	(percent)	(percent)	(percent)
Likeable	87	85	83	80	93
Not very likeable	12	15	9	17	7
Both	1	0	8	3	0

Q 12.   How committed are you to keeping Canada as a country independent of United States?

	(percent)	(percent)	(percent)	(percent)	(percent)
Very Strongly	47	44	42	48	41
Strongly	28	31	29	26	29
Moderate	16	22	21	14	13
Not strongly	4	1	5	4	1
Not committed	5	2	3	8	16

Q 15a.   Do you have a feeling of being a Maritimer

	(percent)	(percent)	(percent)	(percent)	(percent)
Yes	69	71	57	63	55
No	31	29	43	37	45

Q 22c.   Do you think the people here should expect to have the same standard of living as the people in Ontario?

	(percent)	(percent)	(percent)	(percent)	(percent)
Yes	69	77	73	71	79
No	31	23	27	29	21

	New Brunswick			Nova Scotia	
	Non Baptist	Baptist	Franco-phones	Non Baptists	Baptists

Q 32. Overall, would you say Confederation has been a good thing or a bad thing for this province?

	(percent)	(percent)	(percent)	(percent)	(percent)
Good Thing	92	91	92	90	97
Bad Thing	7	6	7	9	3
Both	1	3	1	1	0

Q 35. Do you think the French get better treatment than the English from the government of this province, that the English get better treatment than the French or that the government treats them both about the same?

	(percent)	(percent)	(percent)	(percent)	(percent)
French Treated Better	23	51	2	8	8
English Treated Better	13	7	54	14	5
Both About the Same	64	42	44	78	87

Q 37. Do you think French-speaking people in this province have reason to feel discriminated against?

	(percent)	(percent)	(percent)	(percent)	(percent)
Yes	37	13	56	21	11
No	63	87	44	79	89

Q 38. Do you think French-speaking people in Quebec have reason to feel discriminated against?

	(percent)	(percent)	(percent)	(percent)	(percent)
Yes	30	20	40	32	19
No	70	80	60	68	81

| | New Brunswick | | | Nova Scotia | |
| | Non Baptist | Baptist | Franco-phones | Non Baptists | Baptists |

Q 39a. Do you think the French language and culture contribute to, don't make much difference to or take away from what is good about Canada?

	(percent)	(percent)	(percent)	(percent)	(percent)
Contribute To	74	61	83	74	70
Don't Make Much Difference	18	20	14	18	20
Take Away From	8	19	3	8	10

Q 44b. It should be compulsory for children to learn both English and French in school.

	(percent)	(percent)	(percent)	(percent)	(percent)
Agree	67	51	88	52	40
Disagree	33	49	12	48	60

Q 44c. French Canadians ought to have no more privileges than other ethnic or cultural groups.

	(percent)	(percent)	(percent)	(percent)	(percent)
Agree	73	90	53	79	89
Disagree	27	10	47	21	11

Q 44d. It would be better if everybody in Canada spoke only one language.

	(percent)	(percent)	(percent)	(percent)	(percent)
Agree	25	53	10	32	36
Disagree	75	47	90	68	64

Q 44e. French-speaking people outside Quebec should be able to have their children educated in their own language.

	(percent)	(percent)	(percent)	(percent)	(percent)
Agree	85	66	96	71	83
Disagree	15	34	4	29	17

	New Brunswick			Nova Scotia	
	Non Baptist	Baptist	Franco- phones	Non Baptists	Baptists

Q 44f. Everybody should have the opportunity to learn both English and French in school.

	(percent)	(percent)	(percent)	(percent)	(percent)
Agree	98	98	99	98	99
Disagree	2	2	1	2	1

Q 44g. If a majority of the people of Quebec vote in a free and democratic election to leave Canada, we should allow them to go.

	(percent)	(percent)	(percent)	(percent)	(percent)
Agree	63	74	57	71	69
Disagree	37	26	43	29	31

Q 45a. Do you think more should be done, about the right amount is being done, or too much is being done in the federal government's present policy of bilingualism?

	(percent)	(percent)	(percent)	(percent)	(percent)
Do More	30	10	42	20	18
Doing Right Amount	38	19	59	27	25
Doing Too Much	32	71	9	53	57

Q 46. Do you approve of the principle of official bilingualism?

	(percent)	(percent)	(percent)	(percent)	(percent)
Approve	76	52	97	68	70
Disapprove	24	48	3	32	30

	New Brunswick			Nova Scotia	
	Non Baptist	Baptist	Franco-phones	Non Baptists	Baptists

Q 48.   How much difference do you think it would make to this province if Quebec were to leave Confederation?

	(percent)	(percent)	(percent)	(percent)	(percent)
Very Harmful	52	39	58	38	24
Somewhat Harmful	29	34	26	40	58
Make No Difference	13	19	12	16	18
Somewhat Beneficial	5	8	3	3	0
Very Beneficial	1	0	1	3	0

Q 49.   If Quebec were to leave Confederation, what would you want this province to do?

	(percent)	(percent)	(percent)	(percent)	(percent)
Remain with Canada	65	61	67	69	88
Join the U.S.	14	18	13	14	3
Survive as country on own	3	3	4	4	2
Atlantic Union	14	13	12	12	7
Atlantic region join U.S.	0	0	0	0	0
Atlantic Union in Canada	3	5	2	1	0
Join Quebec	1	0	2	0	0

	New Brunswick			Nova Scotia	
	Non Baptist	Baptist	Franco- phones	Non Baptists	Baptists

Q 73. Now, I have a list of pairs of statements, I would like to know which of the pair best represents your opinion.

(a) Some people should be given respect because of the positions they hold regardless of what you think of them personally.

or

People should only be given respect because of the kind of person they are and not just because of the position they hold.

	(percent)	(percent)	(percent)	(percent)	(percent)
Respect Position	21	19	15	24	27
Respect Person	78	81	85	73	70
Both	1	0	0	3	3

Q 73c. Everybody should have the right to express their views in public no matter what these views might be.

or

Some people's views are so dangerous that they should not be allowed to express them in public.

	(percent)	(percent)	(percent)	(percent)	(percent)
Right to Express Views	74	73	76	74	81
Not Allowed to Express Views	26	27	24	26	19

Q 73e. The Prime Minister and ministers should always have to account to Parliament for what they do – even in times of emergency.

or

In a time of emergency, it is best for the Prime Minister and ministers to take complete control without having to account to Parliament.

	(percent)	(percent)	(percent)	(percent)	(percent)
Accountable	55	62	58	59	59
Not Accountable	45	38	42	41	41

	New Brunswick			Nova Scotia	
	Non Baptist	Baptist	Franco- phones	Non Baptists	Baptists

Q 73f. Sometimes it may be necessary in the interest of national security for the police to do things which are not strictly within the law.

or

There is never any justification for the police to do things outside the law.

	(percent)	(percent)	(percent)	(percent)	(percent)
Police are Above Law	56	58	50	62	69
Never Beyond Law	44	42	50	38	31

Q 75a. I don't think that the government cares much what people like or say.

	(percent)	(percent)	(percent)	(percent)	(percent)
Agree	68	80	72	66	77
Disagree	32	20	38	34	23

Q 75i. Most of our politicians are honest people who try to tell the truth.

	(percent)	(percent)	(percent)	(percent)	(percent)
Agree	61	42	63	68	79
Disagree	38	52	37	32	21
Both	1	6	0	0	0

	New Brunswick			Nova Scotia	
	Non Baptist	Baptist	Franco- phones	Non Baptists	Baptists

Q 76a.   A government that takes the time to involve people in its decisions is the best kind of government – even if it isn't the most efficient.

or

A government which doesn't waste time trying to involve people in its decisions but manages public affairs efficiently is the best kind of government.

	(percent)	(percent)	(percent)	(percent)	(percent)
Involve People	66	53	63	58	71
Efficient	34	44	37	42	29
Both	0	3	0	0	0

Q 76e.   Obedience to government and respect for those in authority are the most important virtues in good citizens.

or

The most important virtues in good citizens are the willingness to question government and the willingness to speak out against those in authority when you believe something is wrong.

	(percent)	(percent)	(percent)	(percent)	(percent)
Obedience and Respect	13	5	29	4	6
Question Authority	86	93	69	95	94
Both	1	1	2	1	0

	New Brunswick			Nova Scotia	
	Non Baptist	Baptist	Franco-phones	Non Baptist	Baptists

Q 77. How much of the time do you think you can trust the government to do what is right?

	(percent)	(percent)	(percent)	(percent)	(percent)
Just About Always	7	8	10	6	3
Most of the Time	46	25	50	42	42
Some of the Time	47	67	40	52	55
Never	0	0	0	0	0

Q 78. Do you have any real control over your ability to achieve the things you want to achieve with your life?

	(percent)	(percent)	(percent)	(percent)	(percent)
Great Deal	50	44	46	47	44
Some	38	39	44	38	45
Not Very Much	12	17	10	15	11

Q 80a. Looking back now on the events of October, 1970, do you think the government was right or wrong to impose the War Measures Act?

	(percent)	(percent)	(percent)	(percent)	(percent)
Right	80	85	77	82	92
Wrong	20	15	23	18	8

Q 90a. What religion were you brought up in?

	(percent)	(percent)	(percent)	(percent)	(percent)
None	1	0	0	3	0
Roman Catholic	61	5	100	39	0
United	13	5	0	19	0
Anglican	12	4	0	18	3
Presbyterian	3	2	0	10	0
Baptist	5	81	0	4	95
Pentecostal	1	0	0	1	0
Other	4	3	0	6	2

	New Brunswick			Nova Scotia	
	Non Baptist	Baptist	Franco-phones	Non Baptists	Baptists

Q 91. Do you think of yourself as being very religious, religious or not very religious.

	(percent)	(percent)	(percent)	(percent)	(percent)
Very Religious	9	11	10	5	8
Religious	65	62	67	58	48
Not Very Religious	26	27	23	37	44

Q 92. Have you ever been positively affected by a religious revival or by the charismatic movement?

	(percent)	(percent)	(percent)	(percent)	(percent)
Religious Revival	7	25	10	6	7
Charismatic Movement	4	1	5	1	3
No	89	72	85	93	90
Both	0	2	0	0	0

Q 93. Have you ever been involved in activities carrying the message of your religion to other people?

	(percent)	(percent)	(percent)	(percent)	(percent)
Yes	13	27	12	12	14
No	87	73	88	88	86

Q 95. How involved are you in activities or groups associated with your church?

	(percent)	(percent)	(percent)	(percent)	(percent)
Very Involved	13	17	17	10	16
Somewhat Involved	26	33	31	26	26
Not Very Involved	61	50	52	64	58

Q 99a. Were you born and raised in this province?

	(percent)	(percent)	(percent)	(percent)	(percent)
Yes	84	88	92	83	92
No	16	12	8	17	8

	New Brunswick			Nova Scotia	
	Non Baptist	Baptist	Franco-phones	Non Baptists	Baptists

Q 100a. In this province, have you always lived in this same community?

	(percent)	(percent)	(percent)	(percent)	(percent)
Yes	63	56	56	58	42
No	37	44	44	42	58

Q 111a What is the highest grade you finished in school?

	(percent)	(percent)	(percent)	(percent)	(percent)
Grade 8 or less	23	28	n/a	19	25
Some High School	21	14	n/a	25	23
High School Matriculation	11	6	n/a	10	0
Vocational	14	15	n/a	15	25
Non-University	15	27	n/a	13	9
Some University	4	0	n/a	6	0
University Degree	12	10	n/a	12	18

Q 112. How old are you?

	(percent)	(percent)	(percent)	(percent)	(percent)
18-29	27	21	n/a	24	17
30-39	21	14	n/a	19	14
40-49	13	9	n/a	12	14
50-59	14	21	n/a	18	15
60-64	7	9	n/a	9	17
65-69	9	13	n/a	7	9
70-79	8	7	n/a	9	8
80 or over	1	6	n/a	2	6

Appendix B

Religion and the Population of Nova Scotia and New Brunswick

Nova Scotia – Origins of Population, 1871 – 1901

Origin	1871	1881	1901
English	113,520 (29.3%)	128,986 (29.3%)	159,753 (34.8%)
Irish	62,851 (16.2%)	66,067 (15.0%)	54,710 (11.9%)
Scotch	130,741 (33.7%)	146,027 (33.1%)	143,382 (31.2%)
Welsh	1,112 (0.3%)	1,158 (0.3%)	1,219 (0.3%)
Indian	1,666 (0.4%)	2,125 (0.5%)	1,629 (0.4%)
French	32,833 (8.5%)	41,219 (9.4%)	45,161 (9.8%)
Dutch	2,868 (0.7%)	2,197 (0.5%)	2,941 (0.6%)
African	6,212 (1.6%)	7,062 (1.6%)	5,984 (1.3%)
German	31,942 (8.2%)	40,065 (9.1%)	41,020 (8.9%)
Others	4,055 (1.0%)	5,666 (1.3%)	3,775 (0.8%)

New Brunswick – Origins of Population, 1871 – 1901

Origin	1871	1881	1901
English	83,598 (29.3%)	93,387 (29.1%)	104,683 (31.6%)
Irish	100,643 (35.2%)	101,284 (31.5%)	83,384 (25.2%)
Scotch	40,858 (14.3%)	49,829 (15.5%)	48,310 (14.6%)
Welsh	1,096 (0.4%)	1,474 (0.5%)	1,147 (0.3%)
Indian	1,403 (0.5%)	1,401 (0.4%)	1,465 (0.4%)
French	44,907 (15.7%)	56,635 (17.6%)	79,979 (24.2%)
Dutch	6,004 (2.1%)	4,373 (1.4%)	3,663 (1.1%)
African	1,701 (0.6%)	1,683 (0.5%)	1,368 (0.4%)
German	4,478 (1.6%)	6,310 (2.0%)	3,816 (1.2%)
Others	906 (0.3%)	4,902 (1.5%)	3,305 (1.0%)

Nova Scotia – Number of Baptists and Percentage of Population, 1827 – 1981

Year	Population	Baptists	Free Will Baptists
1827	123,630	19,790 (16.0%)	—
1851	276,854	42,643 (15.4%)	—
1861	330,857	62,040 (18.8%)	—
1871	387,800	54,263 (14.0%)	19,032 (4.9%)
1881	440,572	73,149 (16.6%)	10,612 (2.4%)
1891	450,396	72,731 (16.1%)	10,377 (2.3%)
1901	459,574	74,869 (16.3%)	8,364 (1.8%)
1911	492,338	83,854 (17.0%)	—
1921	523,837	86,833 (16.6%)	—
1931	512,846	82,171 (16.0%)	—
1941	577,962	89,501 (15.5%)	—
1951	642,584	94,103 (14.6%)	—
1961	737,007	101,093 (13.7%)	—
1971	788,960	100,350 (12.7%)	—
1981	839,800	101,585 (12.0%)	—

New Brunswick – Number of Baptists and Percentage of Population, 1861 – 1981

Year	Population	Baptists	Free Will Baptists
1861	252,047	57,730 (22.9%)	—
1871	285,594	42,729 (15.0%)	27,866 (9.8%)
1881	321,233	49,489 (15.4%)	31,603 (9.8%)
1891	321,263	54,960 (17.1%)	24,674 (7.7%)
1901	331,120	65,206 (19.7%)	15,668 (4.7%)
1911	351,889	82,106 (23.3%)	—
1921	387,876	86,254 (22.2%)	—
1931	408,219	83,880 (20.5%)	—
1941	457,401	88,888 (19.4%)	—
1951	515,697	90,681 (17.6%)	—
1961	597,936	94,070 (15.7%)	—
1971	634,555	89,015 (14.0%)	—
1981	689,370	88,520 (12.8%)	—

Nova Scotia – Religion of Population, 1911 – 1981

Year	Population	No Religion	Church of England	Methodists/ United Church	Salvation Army	Pentecostal	Presbyterian	Roman Catholics	Baptists
1911	492,338		75,315 (15.3%)	57,606 (11.7%)	1,526 (0.3%)	104 (0.0%)	109,560 (22.3%)	144,991 (29.4%)	83,854 (17.0%)
1921	523,837		85,604 (16.3%)	59,069 (11.3%)	2,071 (0.4%)	76 (0.0%)	109,860 (21.0%)	160,872 (30.7%)	86,833 (16.6%)
1931	512,846		88,738 (17.3%)	110,829 (21.6%)	2,665 (0.5%)	637 (0.1%)	48,960 (9.5%)	162,754 (31.7%)	82,171 (16.0%)
1941	577,962		103,658 (17.9%)	124,621 (21.6%)	3,011 (0.5%)	1,853 (0.3%)	47,537 (8.2%)	188,770 (32.7%)	89,501 (15.5%)
1951	642,584		117,602 (18.3%)	141,152 (22.0%)	4,154 (0.6%)	3,275 (0.5%)	42,422 (6.6%)	217,978 (33.9%)	94,103 (14.6%)
1961	737,007		133,247 (18.1%)	163,633 (22.2%)	N/A	4,618 (0.6%)	41,063 (5.6%)	260,104 (35.3%)	101,093 (13.7%)
1971	788,960		135,695 (17.2%)	162,885 (20.6%)	4,755 (0.6%)	6,865 (0.9%)	40,380 (5.1%)	286,320 (36.3%)	100,350 (12.7%)
1981	839,800	34,335 (4.1%)	131,130 (15.6%)	169,605 (20.2%)	4,900 (0.6%)	10,695 (1.3%)	38,285 (4.6%)	310,140 (37.0%)	101,585 (12.0%)

Sources: Census (1911), v. II, p. 2; Census (1921), v. I, p. 572; Census (1931), v. I, pp. 789 – 90; Census (1941), v. I, pp. 714 – 15; Census (1951), v. I, table 39, pp. 3 – 4; Census (1961), v. I, part 3, bulletin 1.3 – 3, table 86, p. 5; Census (1971), v. I, part 3, bulletin 1.3 – 3, table 10, pp. 1 – 2; Census (1981), Advance Information "Population by Selected Religions," p. 17.

New Brunswick – Religion of Population, 1911 – 1981

Year	Population	No Religion	Church of England	Methodists/ United Church	Salvation Army	Pentecostal	Presbyterians	Roman Catholics	Baptists
1911	351,889		42,864 (12.2%)	34,558 (9.8%)	688 (0.2%)	4 (0.0%)	39,207 (11.1%)	144,889 (41.2%)	82,106 (23.3%)
1921	387,876		47,020 (12.1%)	34,872 (9.0%)	736 (0.2%)	218 (0.1%)	41,277 (10.6%)	170,531 (44.0%)	86,254 (22.2%)
1931	408,219		48,931 (12.0%)	61,201 (15.0%)	946 (0.2%)	1,767 (0.4%)	16,260 (4.0%)	188,098 (46.1%)	83,880 (20.5%)
1941	457,401		55,230 (12.1%)	63,355 (13.9%)	1,137 (0.2%)	5,059 (1.1%)	15,403 (3.4%)	220,690 (48.2%)	88,888 (19.4%)
1951	515,697		59,847 (11.6%)	71,879 (13.9%)	1,438 (0.3%)	9,507 (1.8%)	13,323 (2.6%)	260,742 (50.6%)	90,681 (17.6%)
1961	597,936		68,165 (11.4%)	85,710 (14.3%)	N/A	12,059 (2.0%)	13,546 (2.3%)	310,607 (51.9%)	94,070 (15.7%)
1971	634,555		69,260 (10.9%)	85,185 (13.4%)	2,185 (0.3%)	16,895 (2.7%)	13,155 (2.1%)	331,290 (52.2%)	89,015 (14.0%)
1981	689,370	19,685 (2.9%)	66,260 (9.6%)	87,460 (12.7%)	1,965 (0.3%)	21,450 (3.1%)	12,070 (1.8%)	371,100 (53.5%)	88,520 (12.8%)

Sources: Census (1911), v. II, p. 2; Census (1921), v. I, p. 572; Census (1931), v. I, p. 572; Census (1941), v. I, pp. 790 – 1; Census (1951), v. I, table 39, pp. 3 – 4; Census (1961), v. I, p. 715; Census (1971), v. I, part 3, bulletin 1.3 – 3, table 10, pp. 1 – 2; Census (1981), Advance Information "Population by Selected Religions," p. 17.

Index